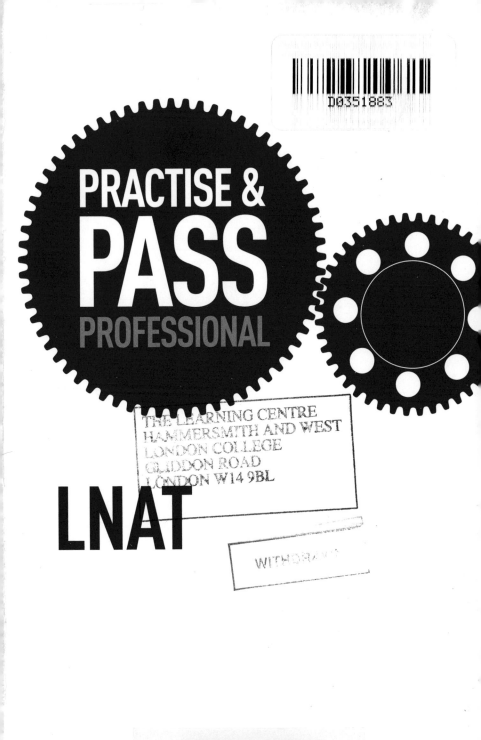

PRACTISE &
PASS
PROFESSIONAL

LNAT

PRACTISE &
PASS
PROFESSIONAL

ACHIEVE YOUR
PERSONAL BEST

LNAT

GEORGINA PETROVA & CHRISTOPHER M. REID

trotman **t**

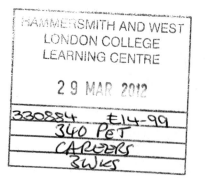
Practise & Pass Professional: LNAT

This first edition published in 2011 by Trotman Publishing, a division of Crimson Publishing Ltd, Westminster House, Kew Road, Richmond, Surrey TW9 2ND

Authors: Georgina Petrova & Christopher M. Reid

British Library Cataloguing in Publication Data
A catalogue record for this book is available from the British Library

ISBN 978 1 84455 383 9

Typeset by RefineCatch Ltd, Bungay, Suffolk
Printed and bound in the UK by Ashford Colour Press, Gosport, Hants

ACKNOWLEDGEMENTS

The authors would like to thank the following for their very kind permissions to reproduce copyrighted material.

Robert Murray Davis and *World Literature Today*, extract from Davis, 'Whatever Happened to Richard Fariña?' 80 *World Literature Today* (2006)

James Hawes and the *Edinburgh Review*, extract from Hawes, 'Repression's Capital, Europe's Canary,' 128 *Edinburgh Review* (2010)

Julia Hell and *Telos*, extract from Hell, 'Remnants of Totalitarianism,' 136 *Telos* (Fall 2006)

Geert Lovink, extract from Lovink, 'myBrain.net' www.eurozine.com/articles/2010-03-18-lovink-en.html

Jakob Norberg and *Fronesis*, extract from Norberg, 'No Coffee,' 24 *Fronesis* (2007)

Claus Offe and *Transit*, extract from Offe, 'Lessons Learned and Open Questions,' 38 *Transit* (2009)

Gillian Rose and *new formations*, extract from Rose, 'Spectacles and Spectres: London 7 July 2005' 62 *new formations* (Autumn 2007)

Elizabeth Siegel Watkins and *new formations*, extract from Watkins, 'Parsing the Postmenopausal Pregnancy: A Case Study in the New Eugenics,' 60 *new formations* (Spring 2007)

In addition, extracts from the following out of copyright texts have been reproduced.

Bagehot, Walter; *The English Constitution* (London, Nelson, 1872)

Bentham, Jeremy; *The Works of Jeremy Bentham* Vol II (Edinburgh: William Tait, 1843)

Brooks, Rupert; in Morley ed. *Modern Essays* (New York: Harcourt, Brace and Co., 1921)

Burke, Edmund; in Eliot ed. *The Harvard Classics* Vol XXIV, Part 3 (New York: P.F. Collier & Son, 1909–14)

Clausewitz, Carl von; Graham trans. *On War* (London: N. Trübner, 1873)

Darwin, Charles; in Eliot ed. *The Harvard Classics* Vol XI (New York: P.F. Collier & Son, 1909–14)

Freud, Sigmund; Hubback trans. *Beyond the Pleasure Principle* (London, Vienna: International Psycho-Analytical, 1922)

Kelvin; in Eliot ed. *The Harvard Classics* Vol XXX (New York: P.F. Collier & Son, 1909–14)

Locke, John; *Two Treatises on Government* (London, 1821)

Mencken, HL; *The American Language: An Inquiry into the Development of English in the United States*, 2nd ed. (New York, AA Knopf, 1921)

Mill, John Stuart; *On Liberty* 4th edn (London: Longman, Roberts & Green, 1869)

Pater, Walter; *The Renaissance: Studies in Art and Poetry* (London: Macmillan, 1877)

Roosevelt, Theodore; *An Autobiography* (New York: Macmillan, 1913)

Smith, Adam; in Eliot ed. *The Harvard Classics* Vol X (New York: P.F. Collier & Son, 1909–14)

Swift, Jonathan; in Eliot ed. *The Harvard Classics* Vol XXVII (New York: P.F. Collier & Son, 1909–14)

CONTENTS

ABOUT THE AUTHORS

GEORGINA PETROVA LL.B (Hons) is a First Class Honours graduate in Law with German Law from University College London and Ludwig-Maximilians-Universität München. She is the 2010–11 Princess Royal Scholar of The Honourable Society of the Inner Temple, and in the summer of 2011 she was called to the Bar at Inner Temple.

CHRISTOPHER M. REID LL.B (Hons) is a First Class Honours graduate in Law from University College London, where he was the winner of the Andrews Medal for the most distinguished graduate in Law. He is a Candidate for the Bachelor of Civil Law at St Hugh's College, Oxford, where he holds a Studentship from the Arts and Humanities Research Council.

FOREWORD BY CITY LAW TUTORS

The National Admissions Test for Law (LNAT), introduced in 2004, was designed to assist the admissions tutors in the UK's leading law schools in identifying the most able students to accept onto their undergraduate law degree programmes. It is a tough test and an important part in a competitive process.

At City Law Tutors we have considerable experience assisting students in preparing for the LNAT. We also run one-on-one LNAT coaching sessions at our tuition centre in Central London. We have produced this book to assist you in preparing for the LNAT. Our aim has been to provide a complete guide to all aspects of the LNAT, from how to register through to detailed preparation for both parts of the test, to next steps and what to expect after the LNAT.

We hope you enjoy this book, that you find it useful, and that you go on to secure a place on the degree programme of your choice.

Good luck!
City Law Tutors

INTRODUCTION

No one can teach you the LNAT.

The LNAT is not a test of knowledge, and it is not something
that you can revise for in the way that you have revised for your
exams up until now. Those qualifications were designed to test
how much you knew about a subject first, and only secondarily
to test your skills - how well you could distinguish or relate
different ideas, for example, or how persuasively you could
formulate an argument. The LNAT is different from anything
you are likely to have encountered because it is exclusively
designed to test a particular set of skills. You will not have to
know anything beyond a broad and general current awareness
to perform well on the LNAT, but you will need to have
developed very well the analytical skills the LNAT rewards. How
then can you prepare?

The purpose of the LNAT is to allow candidates an opportunity
to display what are considered to be the skills which are the
most valuable to a law student: the skills you will use every
day when studying law. Throughout this book the first and
most important thing we aim to do is to explain to you exactly
what those skills are, and to show you how they are applied.
Once you have identified what is being tested and what the
LNAT looks to reward, we will show you how you can improve.
Our guiding principle throughout our explanations is that
trying to teach you how examiners think, or how you can tell

which multiple choice answer is the weakest, or any negative explanation from 'what not to do', is worthless. We aim to tell you positively how to arrive at a correct answer, or a valid conclusion from a given premise, in a structured and developed way. We aim to build your analytical and argumentative skills to give you confidence in your own independent reasoning.

The core of this book is the practice tests we have written, in which we have tried to simulate as closely as possible the standard and feel of the LNAT. Once we have begun our training of your analytical skills, the tests are there for you to measure in practical terms what we mean. After you have taken the tests, each of the multiple choice questions will be taken apart and we will demonstrate not only the correct answer, but most importantly, how you should arrive at that answer and why that particular answer is the correct one. For the exam questions, we will demonstrate the structure, relevance, and argumentative skills that will be expected of you, explaining from the question itself reasoned ways of reaching your conclusions. Our ambition after you complete the book is to put you in a position from which you can naturally improve by continuing the patterns of thought we have illustrated. It is these habits of clear and logical thought that will give you the confidence to successfully realise your potential when taking the LNAT.

The first portion of the book will explain to you what the LNAT is, why you are taking it, and what universities do with the results that you give them. We offer advice on time management and how to approach the test in a calm and prepared way. Our hope is that the instruction that we offer will prove valuable even once you have left the exam room, not only with knowledge of what the next steps are and what to expect, but also to help you to think about the set of skills that you will need in law school and how you can further improve. If after reading the book we have left you thinking more clearly about topical issues, understanding more deeply the views of others, and constructing your own arguments more confidently, you will not only be prepared for success on the LNAT but well advanced in your preparation for starting the study of law.

Before starting the book, it is important to stress that you should not be daunted by the LNAT. Law is hard, and it is true that success in studying it is demanding, intensive and difficult. It is also the most exciting and inexhaustible subject open to you, which offers you a completely new way of understanding the world. The LNAT, however, is not law, and the tough technical skills which you will need to study it will all come later. They will develop naturally with exposure and practice from the basic skills which the LNAT tests and which we set out in this book. That is the value of and the reason for the test, and we hope you are excited about this first step to studying law.

Georgina Petrova
Christopher M. Reid
February 2011, London

CHAPTER 1
WHAT IS THE LNAT?

The National Admissions Test for Law (LNAT) is an exam used by universities in the UK and elsewhere to provide a means of assessment for aspiring law students distinct from their school exam results. The purpose of the test is to examine those skills most necessary for law students, and hence to provide universities with a means of differentiating between candidates who apply to study law. In the words of Dr Liora Lazarus, the LNAT Chair and a Fellow of St Anne's College, Oxford, writing in *The Times* last summer:

'What is needed is what we, a group of the UK's leading university law schools, implemented six years ago: an admissions test running in parallel with the A-level system that gives real results rather than predicted grades; a test that measures raw ability rather than the quality of coaching and education that applicants have received; a test that successfully separates the very best from the very good, regardless of education, background or coaching.'[1]

Detailed advice and guidance on exactly which skills the LNAT tests and the best way to prepare yourself for what the LNAT expects of you will be found in Chapters 3 and 4. The purpose of this chapter is to explain to you the practicalities of the test and the thinking behind it.

BENEFITS OF APTITUDE TESTING

The LNAT is just part of a growing movement in the legal profession towards aptitude testing of one kind or another.

---

[1] Lazarus, Liora: 'Sifting Great Students From the Very Good,' *Times Higher Education* (12 August 2010).

The Bar Standards Board (which among other things has responsibility for regulating admissions to take the professional qualification required for students to become barristers) launched the second pilot of its own aptitude test in 2010, with proposals to make the test compulsory for applicants if the Board continues to think the pilot results are successful. The Law Society and the Solicitors Regulation Authority (the equivalent bodies for solicitors) are also actively considering proposals to introduce aptitude testing for students wishing to take their professional qualification to be entered to the Rolls. The case for introducing these professional tests is far from made out, and there is a great deal of opposition from some quarters to such a move. However, after a controversial start, the LNAT has established its place over the last several years as a useful tool, but just one factor to be taken into account - for selecting students applying for academic degrees in law. There is a genuine and legitimate difficulty experienced by university admissions departments in selecting between equally high-performing applicants in a meaningful way. This is largely because the standard GCSE and A level results do not relevantly separate one candidate from another when it comes to aptitude to study law. It is to this difficulty that the LNAT responds.

Having to sit the LNAT may seem an enormous inconvenience, on top of the many other things you have to do when applying for university. You have to write personal statements; you have to sit interviews; you have to scan transcripts and obtain references; and so on. It may help to think of the LNAT as a very clear opportunity for you to reduce one uncertainty among the many that face you. The LNAT is a clear, well-designed and useful tool upon which, on the whole, university admissions departments set value. It provides them both with an unambiguous result in the form of your score to the multiple-choice questions of Part I of the test, and it provides them with a succinct sample of your written work in the form of your essay answer to Part II of the test. These results, taken as they will be under exam conditions on a single day, help to isolate those students who can perform to a high standard under pressure without the benefit of resit marks or coursework. If you can think of the LNAT as an opportunity for you to demonstrate that you can independently display the skills that a law student will most require, and therefore as an opportunity for you to demonstrate that you have the raw material to succeed in law school, the test should become a challenge rather than a chore, and a chance for you to inject confidence into your application.

WHO HAS TO SIT THE LNAT?

You will be required to sit the LNAT if the university to which you are applying to study law is either a member of the LNAT Consortium or a customer of it. At the time of writing this includes the following UK universities:

- University of Birmingham
- Bristol University
- Durham University
- University of Glasgow
- King's College London
- University of Nottingham
- University of Oxford
- University College London.

The following universities outside the UK also use the LNAT:

- ▶ the National University of Ireland, Maynooth
- ▶ IE University (Madrid and Segovia).

All applicants to read law at these universities are obliged to sit the LNAT by the deadline announced by each university to which you are applying. The deadlines of each university may well be different, so it is crucial that you inform yourself as early as possible of this. Note in particular that the University of Oxford has an especially early deadline - usually some months earlier than other universities. You will of course need to apply to these universities in the usual way, by the procedures which each of them specifies: the LNAT Consortium is quite clear that taking the LNAT 'does not constitute an application to any universities'.[2]

WHEN SHOULD I TAKE THE LNAT?

Different universities have different LNAT deadlines. You are responsible for making sure that you have checked and complied with the relevant deadline for your chosen institution(s). In respect of timing of the LNAT, you are advised to take the test as early in the academic year as feasible in order to maximise your choice of venues and time-slots. Do not underestimate the number of candidates sitting the LNAT each year and make sure that you secure your test-slot well in advance. Once you have booked your test-slot, you can update your LNAT Profile (see below) by rescheduling or cancelling the

---

[2] www.lnat.ac.uk/lnat-exam/admissions-law.aspx.

time and/or venue of your LNAT-sitting. You will not be charged if you reschedule at any time up to 12 noon (UK time) two working days before your scheduled test-slot.

You can only sit the LNAT once a year between 1 September and 30 June. If, contrary to the rules, you sit the LNAT more than once, only the first score will be valid. You must sit the LNAT in the year in which you are applying to university. You can only sit the test once in an application cycle. It is not permissible to use the LNAT scores from a previous year in a later application. This means that if you fail to obtain a place at university and wish to attempt to reapply the year after, you must take the LNAT afresh in order to apply. Make sure that you consult the individual universities before applying.

REGISTERING FOR THE LNAT

Once you have familiarised yourself with the deadlines for application provided by the universities to which you are applying, the next thing to do is to register online. You should do this as soon as you can. Registration is a simple process, and can be completed in a matter of moments at www.lnat.ac.uk/lnat-registration.aspx. Registration will provide you with a list of approved centres close to you where you can sit the test. The official advice emphasises the need to register as early as possible to secure a place at a test centre which is actually close to you; if you leave registration close to the deadline, you may have to travel some distance in order to take the test. Once you have found a suitable test centre, you may then book an appointment to sit the LNAT.

Booking the LNAT

In order to book your LNAT time-slot, there are two steps you have to take. First, you must set up an online account and register your details at www.lnat.ac.uk/registration/create-account.aspx. If you are applying through UCAS, you will need your UCAS Personal Identifier in order to register. When you complete your account you will have an LNAT Profile which will include an LNAT username and password. Second, you must book a test-slot. Upon registration, you will receive an email with the details of how to book and pay for the test. In order to book a test-sitting you should log into your LNAT account and use the navigation menu at the top left of the screen to make a booking. If you require any special arrangements, you should not book the test online but follow the instructions on the LNAT website www.lnat.ac.uk/lnat-registration/common-law-admission-test.aspx. Once you have completed your booking, you will be sent a confirmation email from Pearson VUE, which you should keep and print out in order to bring it to the test centre on the day of your LNAT.

Paying for the LNAT

It costs £50 to sit the LNAT at UK/EU test centres and £70 at test centres outside of the EU. You must pay the fee online when you book the test. The LNAT accepts most major credit cards (Visa, MasterCard, American Express and JCB) and Visa debit cards. Switch/Maestro credit cards are currently not accepted. If you do not have access to a credit card or a Visa debit card, you can apply for an LNAT voucher (for details, see the LNAT website).

INSIDER INFO

LNAT BURSARY SYSTEM

If you are a UK/EU student in receipt of certain state benefits, you may be eligible for waiver of the test fees through the LNAT bursary system. In order to apply for a bursary, you have to download and complete the LNAT Bursary form from the LNAT website. Note that it takes at least 10 working days to process the bursary application, therefore you should ensure that you complete yours in plenty of time in order to allow for your application to be processed before you book and take your test.

THE TEST FORMAT

The LNAT is a computer-based test, which is written and calibrated by Edexcel for Pearson VUE, who format numerous tests and assessments for businesses and educational institutions. In order to take the LNAT, you must attend a designated test centre. There are over 500 such centres in 165 countries around the world, which are fully listed on the LNAT website (www.lnat.ac.uk).

Taking the test

The LNAT lasts 2 hours and 15 minutes and it is divided into two parts. Part I, or Section A, consists of 42 multiple choice questions, which are based on 12 texts, each text carrying three or four verbal reasoning questions (See Chapter 4 for further information). You will be allowed 1 hour and 35 minutes to answer the first part. After you have completed Part I, you must progress on to Part II and you will not be able to return to Part I at the end of the test.

The LNAT divides the two sections in this way because it is intended to allow a precise, albeit relatively generous, amount of time for each section. This ensures that candidates do not attempt to write an essay in 15 minutes as a result of spending too long on the multiple choice questions and that the skills each part intends to test are in fact manifested within sufficient time.

Part II, or Section B, contains a choice of five essay questions out of which you must choose and answer one. You will have 40 minutes to plan and complete your answer (See Chapter 5 for further information). You will be provided with a white board and a marker for the planning of your essay. You will not be permitted any other writing materials and likewise, you cannot submit any handwritten work. The essay itself must be typed and submitted in electronic format.

What to bring on the day

On the day of the LNAT, you must bring with you:

1. photographic identification
2. a printout of your confirmation email from Pearson VUE.

It is essential that you bring a recognised piece of photo ID, because failing to do so will result in an inability to sit the test. As a consequence, you will have to book and pay for a new test slot on another day. Check the LNAT website for a comprehensive list of accepted forms of photographic identification.

PREPARING FOR THE LNAT

Having registered for the LNAT and booked an appointment to take the test, you should begin familiarising yourself with the nature of the test. We have structured the rest of the book to enable you to do this, starting with the basic information about the skills the LNAT tests, and then building your awareness of what is involved in those skills, before taking you step by step through the two parts of the test in detail.

CHAPTER 2
TIME MANAGEMENT

At this stage in your academic life, you will be no stranger to exams and to the idea that you have to make the most of the limited time that you are given. Unfortunately, most of the exams that you will have taken up until this point (and indeed most of the exams that you will take while you are at university) are exercises in performance art more than anything else. They ask a series of questions, and the objective is to display as great a depth and breadth of the relevant knowledge as you can. The freedom this allows you can sometimes mean that knowing what to put in can be an imprecise business. The LNAT is different from this format, but raises problems of its own with regard to time management. We have already illustrated the skills-based rather than knowledge-based nature of the LNAT. How then do you distribute your time across skills?

This problem is to some extent answered for you by the division of the LNAT into two unequal portions. You have a maximum of 95 minutes to spend on Part I's multiple choice questions, and a maximum of 40 minutes to spend on the essay question. You will have to answer 42 questions for Part I and a single question in Part II. If this seems to swing your emphasis one way, recall that Part II contains the only sentences of yours that university admissions will read; they will only see your score from Part I. The solution to the problem is to avoid thinking of time spent on one as necessarily at the expense of the other. You should take the maximum time allowed for each. There are no additional marks available for racing through and finishing as quickly as you can. Speed of analysis is not the objective of the test. Take the time given to you. The more accurate question then becomes, within the maximum time allotted to each part of the test, how should you distribute your time?

PART I: MULTIPLE CHOICE QUESTIONS

It would not make much sense to divide your time *exactly* equally between each question. Though the questions are 'weighted' at a broadly constant level of difficulty, you will find some questions easier than others in accordance with your own strengths and habits of analysis. Don't worry therefore that you will find yourself spending a little longer on some questions. That said, this must be balanced by the need to spend a *roughly* equal time on each question.

Reading the passage

The single most important investment of your time in each section of three or four questions should be reading the passage. This is for the reason that thoroughly reading the passage first, concentrating on understanding its tone, its structure, the priority of the arguments made by the author, will save you time immediately after you have read the questions. This is not to say that having read the questions, you should proceed straight to answering them on the basis of your first reading of the passage. The advantage is that when you are guided to a specific part of the passage by the majority of the questions, you will be able to carefully re-read the *section* which the question pertains to while having in your head a coherent appreciation of how that part relates to the whole passage. This method of devoting the most time per question to reading the passage will avoid you having to re-read the passage as a whole again, which will allow you to devote the proper time to the questions themselves, which should be your next time priority.

Paying attention to the questions

Paying careful attention to the questions should be your second-largest investment of time. While reading the questions, you should ask yourself 'which of the skill categories does this question seek to test'? In Chapter 3, we will discuss in detail a thorough approach to each kind of question within the three broad headings the questions in Part I of the test fall into. It is exactly this approach which you should apply here. Using our shorthand subdivision of the kind of questions you will encounter should make it clear to you what skills the question is testing, and exactly what is expected of you. This will allow you to re-read the relevant section of the passage in a targeted and skills-driven way.

Selecting your answer

Perhaps strangely, selecting your answer from the options with which the question presents you should command the least of your time. This is consistent with the strategy that we aim to suggest to you throughout Chapters 3 and 4 guiding you through the specifics of answering Parts I and II: teaching you to think about the question and to understand exactly the skills being asked of you in such a way so as to enable you to arrive at the answer *positively*, without having to spend time working through which answers are inapplicable. If you apply our method correctly, the vast majority of the work will be done in reading the passage and concentrating on the question, together with re-reading the section of the passage the question pertains to. It is our aim to leave you sufficiently informed about the skills the LNAT rewards that this final stage - selecting an answer - should come naturally to you.

Looking over difficult questions

Once you have completed Part I and submitted, it will not be possible to return to this section. You should make a note as you proceed through Part I therefore of any questions that you found particularly difficult. The final part of your time should not be spent re-reading through the whole of your answers, because this will be too time-consuming; but rather looking over the answers for any question that you found difficult. Though you will not be able to have pen and paper in the exam room, you should make use of the whiteboard and markers which will be provided for you at your desk for this purpose. Discipline yourself to only reviewing those questions that you have marked for review, and marking only those that you genuinely found difficult or had some doubt about. It is simply unrealistic to review every answer, and trying to rush through and do so will sap your confidence.

PART II: ESSAY QUESTIONS

The essay question might appear to present more difficulties to you when it comes to structuring your time. However, once again, applying the methodology we will outline in Chapter 4 should give you the structure onto which you must impose a sensible division of your time. Here, there are a number of differences from our Part I advice above. Firstly, the question itself will demand your close attention, but it will not be the major focus of your time. Neither will your next step - planning your answer and working mentally through the structure you propose to write - though it is again crucial that you devote your next attentions to this. The priority in time management will of course be writing the essay. How should you split your time when doing this?

Planning a structure

It is extremely important to spend 15 minutes creating a structure which sets out your interpretation of the question, the limits of your discussion (that is, elements that you will not consider due to pressure of space, though they would be expected to be included if you had both a greater word count and more time in which to write) and, if possible the ultimate conclusion you will reach. Spending this long within your 40 minute limit on planning may seem excessive, but it is more than justified by the fact that nothing is more effective than a well-organised and structured essay. It immediately tells the reader that you *understand* that it is unrealistic to say anything conclusive within the 40 minute maximum that you are constrained to, and that you know that because of this you have to severely limit yourself. Stating this conclusively at the beginning of your essay is a mark of self-discipline and awareness, and will give you a structure which you can draw upon throughout your answer.

Outline your main points

We then advise you to spend a further 15 minutes on the body of your argument, carefully enumerating your points and spending an equal time on each. It may seem a boring way to write an answer, especially if it is on an interesting or controversial topic, by numbering your arguments, one argument to a paragraph, but this is the single most effective way to ensure that you manage to fit in every argument you wish to make. It is yet another advantage of having invested your time writing an introductory paragraph: by realistically thinking about how many points you have time to make in advance, not only will you be able to plan the time you will distribute over each but you will have the space and the time to develop each satisfactorily.

Conclusion

The final 10 minutes of your time should be spent writing your conclusion. The time spent writing the conclusion should also be the time you spend re-reading what you have written, because you should not be saying anything new in your conclusion. Conclusions are a matter of individual taste; one school of thought says that they are much overrated, and if you haven't anything especially useful to say by way of summary or a concluding point, don't bother writing one. Whatever the merits of this for essay writing technique when you are at university, we would advise that it is worthwhile to include one

INSIDER INFO

GOOD TIME MANAGEMENT

This is crucial to success on both parts of the LNAT. It is, however, quite simple to structure your time in such a way so as to give yourself the greatest chance of effectiveness. The most important thing to impress upon you is the need to appreciate in advance the different demands that each part will place upon you, and the need to structure your priorities differently in each. Once you have thought about the requirements each question has, and the best way to divide your time accordingly, you will find that this focusing of your energy will in itself enable to you to achieve greater success on the LNAT.

in your Part II answer. This is not least because it will give your answer a structured coherence, but summarising the points you have made will also allow you to spend time carefully re-reading what you have already written.

CHAPTER 3

PART I
OF THE LNAT:
MULTIPLE CHOICE
QUESTIONS

This chapter examines in detail the different types of questions you will be faced with when working on Part I of the LNAT. It looks at the skills which these questions aim to test, and gives an explanation of the possible ways to systematically approach the questions to arrive at the correct answer.

All of the questions in Part I follow the same basic multiple choice format, in which you must select one answer from a possible five. It is important to notice at the outset that the skills being tested in this section are very specific, and they fall along a relatively narrow range. Hence, although the questions appear to be extremely varied and pose a wide a variety of problems (an appearance heightened by the choice of texts of different tones, periods and genre) the types of questions being asked fall into three broad categories. First, there are what we will refer to as *argument* questions. These seek to test your ability to comprehend the argument being made, in a number of distinct ways. Second, there are *stylistic* questions. These aim to test your ability to understand the context in which certain language has been used, and the reasons for such use. Third, there are *interpretation* questions. These are designed to test your ability not only to digest the contents of the passage, but to use that understanding to identify what might or might not follow from the passage, or what the assumption upon which the passage is based might be.

These three broad types of questions pose themselves in many different forms, but each time the general structure and the skills tested remain the same. If you can learn to identify exactly what the question is asking of you, this will be a major hurdle to arriving at the correct answer already cleared.

Now we will look at each of the question types in turn.

ARGUMENT QUESTIONS

All of the texts you will be presented with in Part I will exhibit an argument in some form. There might be one strong argument running throughout the extract, or there may be a number of disparate arguments being made. These questions test your ability to understand *what it is* that the author of the text is arguing. This can be a difficult skill to acquire, because the question tests your ability to understand *what is not* being argued just as much as your ability to understand what *is* being argued. However, once you appreciate the skill being asked of you, all these questions require is a close attention to the whole of the passage, and the exact language used. Argument questions present themselves in Part I in several ways, but all of them are different methods of testing the same central skill of comprehending exactly what is being argued.

Argument identification

These questions are concerned exclusively with what is and what is not being argued in the passage. You are being asked to identify the argument the author makes on the theme that the question will prompt you to. You are not concerned with the separately tested skills of inference, implication or allusion. The multiple choice format of the LNAT tends to mean that these questions break down into positive and negative phrasings. Examples of positive phrasings are:

'The writer takes the view that. . .'

or

'The writer suggests/argues that. . .'

Examples of negative phrasings are:

'The writer does not argue that. . .'

or

'The writer does not suggest that. . .'

Argument identification is a crucial skill for law students. It can be very easy to follow the theme or spirit of an author's writing and yet conclude with a proposition that the writer did not make. A useful distinction to have in mind when looking at these questions and reading the extracts in Part I of the test is the distinction between strong and weak claims. All arguments make claims of some kind. Strong claims are broader and encompass more territory than weak claims, for example, 'The economic unity that the euro represents necessarily entails political unity in the European Union' is a strong claim. Weak claims are more narrow and more limited, 'The economic unity that the euro represents clearly has some political consequences in the European Union' is a weak claim. In the multiple choice options which the question has given you, consider which of the categories of strong or weak claim the options fall into. Start with the strong claims. Does the passage really contain this argument? This will allow you to focus more easily on exactly what is being said, and eliminate arguments that are not being made at all.

Argument application

These questions test your ability to apply in a limited context the core argument being made in the passage. Based on the conclusions of the argument, you will be asked to apply it to a new situation. It is important to recognise that you are not being asked to go beyond the terms of the argument or of anything contained within the passage. Specifically, you are not being asked *what might follow* from the argument in the passage. You are being asked to apply what *is* in the passage to *this* situation. For example, if the argument in the passage concerned 'Y'.

'Based on the passage, why might X be against Y?'

Once again, these questions do not test anything other than your understanding of the author's conclusions about 'Y'. The multiple choice options you are given are structured in such a way so as to test your comprehension of the argument by means of its application. The best advice that can be given for approaching these questions therefore is to not be distracted by the idea of application. Concentrate first on correctly identifying the precise argument that the author is making, and then determine whether its scope covers the option you are being presented with.

Argument characterisation

These questions test your ability to reformulate the author's argument to a limited extent in terms which are not the author's own. The skill tested is how far you can *translate* your understanding of the argument into different terms while still maintaining the same meaning. This is again primarily a test of comprehension, but the LNAT does indirectly test your wider understanding of the meaning of words and phrases. These questions present themselves in a wide variety of forms, but all are driving at testing the central skill of conveying understanding in an environment not original to the author:

'Which of the following comes closest to the meaning of X?'

or

'Which of the following best describes the argument that the author makes about X?'

You will also find these questions in a negative formulation. For example:

'Which of the following is not an accurate characterisation of the main argument the author makes about X?'

Here again the distinction between strong and weak claims will help you to arrive at the correct answer. When applying terms which are not the author's to capture his argument, first characterise the specific argument which you have identified the author as making from the passage as a strong or a weak claim. Then, relate this characterisation to the options which you are given. An option which suggests a stronger claim than the author himself makes cannot be the correct answer; neither can an unduly weak expression of the author's point. This should only be a preliminary step in your analysis, but it will help you to focus on the nature of the propositions the options are presenting you with. On this basis, you should then think through your understanding of the argument being made in the passage, and select the option which *best translates* that meaning; that is, the option which best expresses the same claim that the author makes in terms which, though different, convey the same meaning.

STYLISTIC QUESTIONS

All of the authors of the extracts which you will read in Part I of the test have made certain decisions about how they wish to express themselves and advance the argument they wish to make. The whole of an individual passage will exhibit those decisions in the style in which it is written, and the way in which language is used. This is the *context* created by the passage. Stylistic questions will test your understanding of this context by asking you about the contextual meaning of certain words, or the reasons why certain expressions appear as they do, or the function which certain language plays in the passage. Just as we saw in the argumentative questions, however, these diverse kinds of questions all test the same set of skills. All stylistic questions in Part I aim to test how far you have understood the passage as a whole, in the context the author has built up, and how far you can use that understanding to explain specific features of the passage. This is both a narrower and a broader skill than was involved in the argumentative questions. It is narrower because it requires you to think very carefully about isolated sections of text. It is broader in that it requires you to take into account the tone and feel that the author has created in the passage. Though stylistic questions require a certain sensitivity to language, once again we can be much helped by simply identifying the kinds of questions which fall under this category.

Stylistic evaluation

These questions are concerned with meanings peculiar to the individual passage. Authors may use words in a particular and even unusual way, but which nevertheless is perfectly understandable in the context of the passage as a whole. This is especially the case for the texts from different periods of history which appear in Part I. These questions can phrase themselves in a number of ways. For example:

'Which of the following words is used to convey approval?'

or

'The writer here uses the word X to mean. . .'

Alternatively, the question will phrase itself by giving the interpretative meaning it asks you to identify in the passage:

'In which of the following sentences does the writer use irony?'

The purpose of these questions is to test your understanding of how language can be used within a wider framework. Very often as a law student words will be divorced from their ordinary meaning and you will be required to ascertain precisely what meaning is intended to be conveyed. The best strategy for approaching these questions is to read through the passage several times, not only following the argument but also concentrating on the feel and tone of the extract. It will always be clear from the passage as a whole what the meaning or the sense you are being asked to identify is. It is never the case that you must deduce it from the topic itself or what you might know about the wider theme. Concentrate simply on how the author is expressing himself in the particular part you are guided to, and relate that part to the whole passage. Given what has preceded this word, what meaning has the author attributed to it? Given the argument of the author, in what sense is this sentence meant?

You should always be alert to instances of sarcasm, irony or understatement in this category of questions. A definition of the feel of these senses is difficult to set out in advance, so the best way to proceed - either when the question invites you to look explicitly for such moods or when you think the meaning that you are being asked to identify is captured by these senses - is to ask if the particular extract fits the context of the passage as a whole if taken literally. When Jonathan Swift writes about the weight of children, 'I have reckoned upon a medium that a child just born will weigh 12 pounds, and in a solar year, if tolerably nursed, increaseth to 28 pounds', it is clear when he continues that his meaning does not fit if taken literally: 'I grant this food will be somewhat dear, and therefore very proper for landlords, who, as they have already devoured most of the parents, seem to have the best title to the children'.

The most important technique in this kind of question therefore is first gaining an understanding of the sense and feel of the passage as a whole, then analysing the particular extract the question refers you to with this wider contextual feel in mind.

Stylistic explanation

These questions aim to test your understanding of what *function* words or phrases play in the construction of the passage and the advancement of the argument that the author makes:

'Which of the following pairs of words are not used as an opposition in the passage?'

or

'All the following words advance the argument, except. . .'

Once again, this requires you to have absorbed the particular qualities of the passage that make up the context in which the words or phrases you are being asked to comment on appear. This is especially important in stylistic explanation questions because often the *function* a certain phrase plays is linked not only to the kind of text you are considering as a whole, but also to certain positions in the text. For example, texts which give indications of having been originally delivered as speeches might rely heavily on the repetition of certain phrases to advance the argument; texts which throughout have advanced one point of view might use certain qualifying phrases towards the end to introduce a contrary viewpoint. Typically 'argumentative' words such as 'therefore,' 'however,' or 'nevertheless' should in general play significant roles in such an analysis. The focus of these questions is not so much to ascertain the meaning of the words or phrases in themselves, but to identify the work they do in the overall scheme of the author's presentation. This requires close attention to individual words, and the best approach is always to identify clearly to yourself where the author's points begin and end, together with which sections of the passage are not argumentative. Once you have done this, you will have an appreciation of the structure of the passage, and once this structure is isolated it will become much easier to work out the words and phrases which comprise it.

INTERPRETATION QUESTIONS

These questions test your ability to go beyond the terms and framework of the argument to a limited extent. They are concerned with what might either immediately *follow from* the argument advanced in the passage, or what is immediately *prior to* the argument in the passage; that is, what the argument seems to be based on. These questions make up only a small proportion of the questions in Part I, but it is important to appreciate how they work both for their own sake and to have it clearly in your mind how these questions differ from the other categories of questions which we have identified. For example:

'Which of the following is implied but not stated by X?'

This category of questions requires a two-step basic inquiry. First, you must clearly identify the argument which is explicitly being made, using the techniques we discussed earlier with regard to the argument identification category. Second, you must think in terms of *consistency*, so of the options given by the question, which (though not stated in so many words) is *consistent* with the text the question refers you to? Any answer which simply repeats the argument in the passage is incorrect, and this is the crucial difference of the skills tested by this category of question from the other two we have identified.

Once answers which are consistent with the argument advanced in the part of the passage you are referred to have been identified, to arrive at the correct answer you need to determine, depending on what the question may ask, what is *implied* by the text, or what *follows* from the text, or what *assumption* the text makes. These answers outside of the passage can be arrived at by thinking in terms of what is most consistent with the argument which has been advanced. After that, it is in each case a matter of ordinary logic for you to arrive at the correct answer.

This chapter has tried to break down the three different kinds of questions which Part I of the LNAT presents you with. In doing so, we have tried to make the point that understanding what it is that the question is asking you is the vast majority of the work in arriving at the correct answer. Once you have established what the different kinds of question are looking for and the methods they want you to employ in arriving at the answer, the 42 different questions in Part I of the test become vastly more manageable. Take your time in reading this chapter over once again before you attempt the practice tests. Once you have understood the skills Part I of the LNAT seeks to test, you are ready to sit a practice paper.

CHAPTER 4
PART II
OF THE LNAT:
THE ESSAY

Part II of the LNAT presents you with a choice of five essay questions from which you will select and answer one question in 40 minutes. Your answer should be no longer than 500 to 600 words. You will appreciate that this is a very limited space within which to write a full argument. In fact, it should not take you more than 20 minutes to type up your essay once you have planned precisely what to say (see Chapter 2 Time management). Top marks are not the result of the length of your essay, but marks will come from structure, clarity, quality of argument, and most importantly, from the persuasive value of your essay.

We advise you to spend at least 15 minutes planning your essay. The rest of the time should be divided between typing your essay, reading your answer and making any necessary stylistic amendments or additions to the text. Planning is an essential aspect of your essay and will allow you to structure your arguments paragraph by paragraph in a way which flows and which gives you the opportunity to assess what you have included. In this chapter, we will focus on the three key aspects on which you should concentrate in order to make your essay coherent and compelling. These are knowledge (A), structure (B), and persuasiveness (C).

KNOWLEDGE

As you already know, the LNAT is not a test for which you can study. This does not mean that you cannot and should not prepare: it is your skills and not your knowledge that are being tested. This is especially true when you are answering the questions in Part I of the test. Part II, on the other hand, though it focuses on the skill of written argument, necessarily requires a certain level of knowledge of the topic raised by the question. Think of this knowledge as the basic raw material needed to show your skills of building up a sophisticated argument - it is a means to an end rather an end in itself. Your essay will not receive high marks purely for presentation of knowledge on the issue in question, but without some knowledge you will be unable to construct a full and convincing essay.

What kind of knowledge do I need to answer the LNAT essay question?

The kind of knowledge necessary to answer an LNAT question with success is of a general nature and can be acquired through reading a good quality newspaper. You can do this easily enough, but to be effective it must be for longer than the week preceding the test. Your chances will be significantly improved if you can sit the exam with a solid base of information, because this will both expand the choice of questions you can answer and will give you sufficient raw material out of which to carve a compelling argument. We advise you to develop the habit of reading a good quality newspaper on a daily basis. Additionally, you may find it useful to collect articles of interesting events and stories. This approach is preferred by students for two reasons. First, collecting is easily done if you read newspapers electronically as you can simply create a folder with pdf articles. Second, having a database of articles will permit you to review the development of a particular storyline before going into the exam and will allow you to revise on events which struck you.

INSIDER INFO

TACKLING THE ESSAY QUESTION

Note that our guidance on how to answer the essay question (see pages 109–191) includes a list of points which you may choose to consider when tackling the practice questions. Whilst we have focused our questions on topical issues, the guidance is merely a bouquet of ideas and salient points by way of example; it is not a list of topics for you to learn. We have deliberately stayed away from giving sample answers in order to avoid the danger of appearing prescriptive either in substance or in form. Your essay will always be plausible and forceful if you use knowledge with which you have familiarised yourself and can substantiate with recent examples of your own.

How do I choose an essay topic?

When helping students prepare for the LNAT, one of the questions which we are asked most often is how to prepare for the problems presented by the essay question (for further advice, see Chapter 2). We have just advised an approach of developing the habit of reading a good quality newspaper on a regular basis and collecting the articles which you find important. But this advice may seem unhelpful, because the difficulty which many students face at this stage is that they often do not know what is important for the purposes of the test. Generally, it is useless to try to predict which topics will come up because the LNAT questions are designed to be sufficiently broad so as to be unpredictable.

The best answer to the problem of 'importance' is to develop the idea that the type of material which counts as 'LNAT material' is the core of what we might call 'current affairs'. This certainly comprises *news* articles which concern topics like the economy and politics, both domestic and international. It also comprises *debates* and controversies concerning justice, education, health, and communication and information technology. We intend our approach to the LNAT to be holistic in the sense that it aims to complement your overall preparation for reading law and, in this light, we strongly recommend that you use the occasion of sitting the LNAT to develop the habit of keeping yourself thoroughly informed of current affairs. This will help you contextualise your learning once you commence your studies in law.

STRUCTURE

Once you have the necessary knowledge as raw material, the next important skill you need to master is the ability to structure an argument coherently and in a manner which shows your argument in its best light. It is surprising and disappointing how many law undergraduates continue to fail to structure their arguments and miss out on marks because of it. The purpose of the LNAT essay is to test your ability to argue in written form. You are marked on the structure and persuasiveness of your essay. The two go hand in hand. If the examiner cannot easily gather what your arguments are by skimming through your paper, then it is unlikely that he will spend a lot of time trying to detect what it is you have tried to say. The tip to remember is that although the essay is the part of your LNAT which does not get marked, it is the *only* piece of your writing which universities will have access to as evidence of your written abilities. Therefore you should make it easy for the admissions officer to catch the thread of your argument and see quickly and clearly how you have divided your answer. You may come up with very pertinent and potent points, which can easily become lost in a piece of writing which is lacking in structure and thus loses the marks it deserves. Do not let this happen to your essay - structure meticulously.

How to structure your answer

The bulk of your time should go to planning your answer: at least 15 minutes out of 40. This includes structuring what you will say and which paragraph you will say it in. The two areas in which students make the most errors are:

1. understanding what the question is asking
2. answering the question being asked.

Showing that you have interpreted the *scope* of the question correctly and that you have addressed the ambiguities within it count for a lot of points. Structuring your answer will take place in two parts. The first part is concerned with your understanding of the question and addressing its scope appropriately and with respect to your knowledge of the subject matter. The second part is stylistic and is concerned with structuring your answer to the question and deciding tactically which arguments are your strongest and which are the strongest arguments against you.

THE FIRST TASK: UNDERSTANDING THE QUESTION AND ADDRESSING ITS SCOPE

For the first part of the structuring process, we suggest a loose structure which will allow you to show clearly that you have understood the question and that you have answered it clearly. Please note that this structure will not be appropriate as an answer to all questions, but for the purposes of planning, it will allow you to appreciate the different aspects of most questions. Ask yourself the following four questions:

1. **What?**

2. **Why?**

3. **What if?**

4. **What if not?**

Once you have done this, it should be clear to you what the question is asking of you and where the difficulties within any answer lie. Think of the little questions above as the bones of your argument, because they contain the factors which will give shape to it. Let's consider the contents of each structural question.

What?

This is the first question you will ask yourself after you read the question. Ask yourself, *what is* the motion put forth by the question? Then: what is *unclear* about the motion as put forth by the question? Finally, what are the *parameters* of the motion as set out?

This is important for two principal reasons. First, most LNAT questions address a motion of political, economic or ethical significance. The questions will test your ability to recognise what the motion is and what its scope is as worded by the question. It is therefore important to show that you are able to deal with this clearly and as part of your answer. Second, the LNAT questions tend to be sufficiently broad to allow you to set your own parameters to your answer. Remember that you have a very limited space within which to make your argument, so be sure to identify what these parameters will be. You are effectively given the opportunity to set the rules so be sure not to miss it!

For example, let's look at Question 4 in Practice Test 1, Part II (page 116) which asks you to 'critically examine the reasons for and against introducing proportionate representation in the UK'. One way of answering the 'what?' part of your structure is to identify what proportionate representation is. Second, you may consider that there are a number of different notions of proportionate representation and there is more than one model proposed in the UK. You will thereby demonstrate your understanding of the *ambiguities* in the question and a tactical approach to its answer.

Why?

The second question is probably the most important one for the purposes of the LNAT. This is because it propels you through the reasons for and against the motion as you have defined it in the first stage of your structure. In other words, once you have presented your understanding of the question and its scope, you must consider the reasons behind both its positive or negative answer. Additionally, once you have fully identified the reasoning behind the motion, you will have a pretty good picture of how to go about structuring your written answer. There are numerous ways of doing this successfully. Hopefully, by the time you sit the LNAT you will have absorbed sufficient knowledge from your reading to allow you to put forth both sides of the argument and to also take a stance on which side of the argument is most convincing. We do not propose to teach you in this book how to critically reason for the purposes of the LNAT. Ideally, this is a skill with which your sixth-form studies have made you familiar. Nevertheless, some of the questions you may wish to ask yourself include:

- What is the purpose of the change proposed by the statement?
- What might be some of the evidence to suggest that the statement included in the question is accurate?
- What might be the evidence to suggest it is inaccurate?
- What are the interests engaged by the scope of the question?
- Are those interests adequately represented under the status quo?

Note that depending on the motion, the process of questioning yourself will vary. The role of these questions is just to help you catch all the possible reasons to which the argument may give force and to subsequently allow you to evaluate the strength of each for the purposes of your answer.

How?

The third question you will ask yourself addresses the practicalities of the question's motion. There are LNAT questions which will not engage this type of further reasoning. For example, Question 2 in Practice Test 2, Part II (page 183) asks you to give your reasoning in respect of whether assisted suicide should be made lawful. Once you have considered all the interests engaged in legalisation, it is important to consider the practicalities of enforcing those interests, e.g. if suicide were legalised, how would the law monitor its proper implementation without overlooking the obvious detriment to those in a weak physical state who are being assisted to die against their wishes?

What if . . . ? / What if not . . . ?

We will address the third and fourth questions collectively because they involve a very similar exercise. Depending on the question, you may choose to address them separately for the tactical reasons of advancing your argument. Both 'What if . . . ?' questions direct your attention to considering the alternative scenario to the motion you are advancing. In essence, it allows you to show your reader the benefit to be reaped of the practical implication of your argument and the detriments to be suffered if your argument does not succeed. Speculating about the potential effect of a motion can be a very effective rhetorical device for persuading because it does not require hard evidence, merely plausible analogies by way of which to capitalise on the reasons already given. The same caveat applies here as in our discussion of 'How?' in that it may not always be appropriate to focus on practicalities in answering certain questions which call for a more abstract answer. Nevertheless, there will be LNAT questions which will call for this type of reasoning in your argument.

For example, Question 5 in Practice Test 1, Part II (page 119) asks you to discuss the statement that 'In light of the recent financial crisis, the UK has nothing to lose by adopting the euro'. In order to make your argument stronger you may very well like to take into account the likely benefits and disadvantages which will be engaged by the adopting of the euro. This will allow your reader not only to appreciate that you have taken into account the further implications of the statement but allows them to be convinced on yet another ground.

THE SECOND TASK: STRUCTURING YOUR ANSWER AND MAKING TACTICAL DECISIONS

Because structure is such a crucial part of focusing your thoughts and constructing a successful essay, in this book we have dealt with structure in two parts. 'The first task' dealt with structure for the purposes of understanding the question and planning your answer. 'The second task' progresses with the stylistic aspects of structuring your answer. There are a number of ways in which to successfully present an argument. Our purpose here is to make a number of suggestions which you may choose to adopt in order to style your points in the most logical and readable way. We will focus on three essential aspects in the anatomy of your essay:

1. its introduction
2. the components of your essay's body in the form of paragraphs
3. its conclusion.

The introduction

The introduction is one of the easiest ways to impress your reader from the beginning. And yet so few students succeed in taking full advantage of the opportunity it presents. In our experience, this is because students are not ruthless enough in following through with the purpose of the introduction (see Chapter 3). The purpose of the introduction is to allow you to tell the reader what issue or motion the question is addressing; to define the ambiguities in the question; to put forth the scope of your answer; and finally, to enumerate the points you will be making.

We have already discussed how to go about interpreting the question, its ambiguities and the scope of your answer. The stylistic point which you must include in your introduction remains a list of your essay's arguments. Think of this as the roadmap you give your reader. For example, if you state that there are five principal arguments against making assisted suicide lawful, then you would be expected to make those five points in the body of your argument. You may find this approach a little too dull. It is important to appreciate that you are writing an argumentative essay in a very limited amount of space and time - the crucial force of persuasion will come from brevity, strong structure and clear relevance. When a barrister appears in court, like you, he often hasn't had much time to read the brief, and also does not have much time in which to make his case. He must employ similar devices to those you will be using. There isn't a judge in the country who doesn't appreciate an advocate who clearly states in *advance* how much he will say on each issue. Your task in the second part of the LNAT is akin to written advocacy. Think of your reader as a judge or your opponent in court and make sure you tell them where your argument is going and how it is going to get there before diving into the intricacies of your reasoning. If you can do this, your introduction will gain you marks before you even start your argument.

Paragraphs: the organs of the written body

Once you have outlined your arguments, it is time to make them. In the 'Why?' stage of your planning structure you will very likely have gathered a list of reasons for and against the particular argument you will choose to make. In order to make out your case, we suggest you pick the strongest three or four. Remember that your time is limited and it is your skills of argumentation and not thoroughness that are being tested. Therefore, prioritise. Tactically, it is more advantageous to have three strong reasons which are well argued than six weak points which can be rebutted lightly.

Next, we suggest that you dedicate one paragraph to one reason. The totality of reasons will make out your whole argument. It is in this respect that the paragraphs are the organs of your essay. We recommend that you follow through with our advice on the introduction and that you commence each paragraph with the corresponding number of the reason given, in the style 'firstly. . .' and 'secondly. . .'.

INSIDER INFO

USING THE PARAGRAPH STRUCTURE

If we had to give a single tip to an LNAT candidate, this would be it. The enumeration and clear paragraphing approach ensures that your reader knows precisely where they are in your argument and makes it that much easier for them to appreciate each and every point you have made.

Each paragraph should be structured to contain one reason which is followed through and argued compellingly. In the third skill in our discussion (persuasiveness) we will discuss precisely how to weave your argument in the most convincing and potent manner so that it can stand up to scrutiny. For the purpose of structure however, you must ensure that a paragraph is dedicated to each reason and that each reason addresses the points which can be made against it. Dedicating a whole paragraph ensures that you have space to anticipate any points which may be made against you and rebut them so as to convince your reader conclusively.

The conclusion

Writing a conclusion to a well-structured and argued essay can be a very gratifying experience. This is because a conclusion will allow you to appreciate the arguments you have made, mirror your introduction in showing that you have addressed the points discussed therein, then repeat your final argument, or the result of your reasoning, one more time. A well-written conclusion will not mention anything new, but will reiterate the strongest points of the essay, thereby giving it symmetry and style. Because a conclusion will not include any new information, we briefly suggest three tips for writing it.

1. First, the conclusion should be short and strong. Make sure that you include your three strongest arguments. If you can summarise your case in three sentences, your reader will be impressed.

2. Second, make sure that your conclusion concludes your answer to the question asked. This is a good opportunity for you to relate your reasoning to the question asked and to bring all your arguments within the scope of the question.

3. Third, do not worry about saying anything witty or punchy. Make sure you end on a strong note and do not worry about giving your essay the spin of a great thesis. Simply make your point succinctly and end your reasoning in a controlled but forceful manner.

PERSUASIVENESS

The last key aspect of the LNAT essay is its ability to persuade. As we have often repeated, the purpose of the LNAT is to ensure that you have the skills required of a law student. Part I of the test assesses your skills of verbal reasoning and analysis. Part II tests your ability to put forth a positive case and to convince your reader of a pre-determined issue. For this reason, we advise that you develop a broad understanding of a number of topics within current affairs instead of an in-depth knowledge of only a few. Due to the scarcity of time and the general breadth of the questions, persuasiveness can serve as your compass in writing your essay. Remember at all times that the purpose of your essay is to persuade the reader of your answer. Your knowledge and, indeed, your structure, are both the means to this end. The content of your essay should be directed at convincing the reader of your answer, whether you are taking a stance within a polarised argument or you are discussing a controversial statement.

Most students ask at this stage whether they should take a side in the argument. The answer to this is unequivocally yes. So long as your stance falls within the scope of the question, you should use it as the starting point for making your main argument and structure your essay in a way which follows from its premise. It is important to appreciate at this stage that argumentative writing does not mean that you should ignore the arguments against you. It is often said that the case people find most persuasive is the case told from one side only. This may very well be true, but unfortunately in a legal context your audience generally has an interest in determining the case against you! This is a difficulty you can address by including within your argument the arguments against it. We suggest that you start with a positive argument in your favour, develop it, and then consider the argument which can be made against it. Then, show the weaknesses of this opposing argument. Here are the steps for you to remember.

▶ Make a positive argument in favour of your case.
▶ Explain it, and if you can, use an example.
▶ Address the strongest point against it.
▶ Show the weaknesses of this point.
▶ Conclude the paragraph by summing up the positive argument and how it is superior to the argument against it.

There are five principal reasons why we undergo this rigorous exercise with respect to the content of each paragraph.

1. You begin with a positive case which shows that there are positive reasons why your approach is to be preferred. This is especially important if you are making out a case for one outcome directly opposed to another.

2. You contextualise your argument by giving an example of its accuracy, thereby also demonstrating your knowledge of how the argument would operate in practice.

3. By recognising the strongest arguments against you, you show that your argument does not exist in a vacuum and you have given thought to some of the more sophisticated challenges to your reasoning.

4. By succinctly rebutting the strongest argument you will directly show that you have tested the strength of your point and found that it is stronger than the points which may be raised against it. This is an effective method because even if your case as a whole is not perfect, it allows you to present your case as stronger than other possible solutions and therefore as the better option.

5. By concluding on a positive note, your essay will demonstrate your ability to present each argument symmetrically and to 'fold in' any incompatible reasoning in a harmonious and persuasive manner. This will impress your reader both in style and substance.

INSIDER INFO

FINAL REMARK ON THE LNAT ESSAY

We would like to remind you that the essay is generously timed and allows ample room for planning and structuring your answer. This advice translates into the style in which you write your essay. We have touched on the essay's purpose of persuading so far as substance is concerned, but we have not addressed you on the style of your writing. This is because everyone has a different manner of expression and your essay should sound like your writing and not a sample answer. That said, keep in mind that your goal is to convince the reader and not to charm them with elaborate prose. Do not use many words when few will do. Express your points boldly, without hesitation, but do not overstate your case. And lastly, make sure that your writing is convincing in its form – there is plenty of time to ensure that your essay has no spelling, grammar or punctuation mistakes. Do not allow a great argument to be undermined by a mistake which can be easily corrected.

PRACTICE TEST 1

PART I:
MULTIPLE CHOICE QUESTIONS

PRACTICE TEST INSTRUCTIONS

This section is divided into 12 subsections; each subsection has between three and four questions.

You should answer **all** 42 multiple choice questions in Part I (Section A), selecting **one** of the possible answers listed for each question.

Time allowed: 95 minutes

1. NEWSPAPERS AND PHOTOGRAPHY

It has to be said that looking again, differently — indeed, the act of looking at all — was remarkably unproblematised in the British newspapers after the bombs. The emphasis in all the papers immediately after the attacks was on eye-witness accounts, the reliability of which was never questioned. There was also an enthusiasm for the photos sent in to websites (particularly the BBC news website) from survivors' mobile phones, for their immediacy and authenticity; most papers printed phone photos of people walking along the underground tunnels away from the bombed trains. The papers were also struck by the missing posters that appeared on the walls at Kings Cross station, noting that these copied the posters that appeared after the plane attacks on the World Trade Center in 2001 and after the tsunami in December 2004. Although the technology and formats of photography were acknowledged to be changing, then, nonetheless these were all photos being used in the time-honoured tradition of photojournalism, as seemingly transparent windows onto the world, turning those of us who weren't there into apparent witnesses of places and people. Yet despite this lack of reflexivity, and despite all their work of fixing, incorporating and disposing, some of the newspaper photographs do hint at ways of looking responsibly that don't erase the specificity of those killed by the bombers or make the images that tell of their death so unproblematic.

This is the case for two reasons, both to do with the specificity of newspapers as a certain kind of media. First, newspapers work with a different temporality from other news media. Several commentators have noted the importance of speed, immediacy, and being 'live' to both TV and web news reporting. Newspapers, in contrast, now very rarely break news. Instead, they offer description but, more importantly, reaction and analysis to things that have already happened, and about which they often assume their readers will already know the bare facts. Newspapers thus occupy a somewhat more reflective position in relation to events than do screen-based media. The still images that they carry, then, also allow a different relation between spectator and photo than do photographs on a screen. They allow the possibility, at least, of pausing, reflecting, and looking again at what you've already seen.

Secondly, newspaper photos do indeed show us things, which we can then respond to in various ways. And some of the photographs carried by the newspapers after the bombings last July show me a very different relation to photographs than the one the newspapers themselves were enacting. On 23 July, page 9 of the *Daily*

Express carried a photograph of the funeral of David Foulkes, who was buried the previous day in Oldham, near Manchester. It suggests a quite different relation to a photograph than the one used in the press. It showed his girlfriend crying, and holding a large framed photo of him, face out and obscured by her arms. This was not a photo acting as a window onto the world. It looked much more like a tangible memory of something irrevocably lost. It wasn't on display, it was not being looked at and could not be; but it was being held, tightly. And this wasn't the only photo of a photograph being held rather than looked at that the papers printed. There were many others, particularly of friends and family with photos of the missing people they were searching for immediately after the attacks.

1 In the first paragraph, by claiming that newspapers showed a lack of 'reflexivity', the writer is:

(a) suggesting that newspapers are not reliable reporters of fact;
(b) pointing out that photographs can give misleading impressions;
(c) concerned at the newspapers' absence of self-understanding of photographs;
(d) debating whether newspapers might distort photographs they show;
(e) showing that photographs only have one point of view.

2 In the second paragraph, what is the *significance* that the writer sees in the 'more reflective' position of newspapers as opposed to other media?

(a) because they rarely break news, we can be more objective about their reporting;
(b) because of their emphasis on analysis, we can gain a better understanding of the news from newspapers than from other media;
(c) because of their distance from the event, we can be made to feel uncomfortable by the photographs they carry;
(d) because of their distance from the event, we might look differently at newspaper photographs than those carried by other media;
(e) because we can pause to look at newspaper pictures, we won't be distracted by other information.

3 When the writer claims that photographs may be used as *'seemingly* transparent windows onto the world', which may turn those looking at the pictures into *'apparent* witnesses of places and people', what is the point that the writer makes by using these qualifiers?

(a) it is impossible for photographs to do these things;
(b) although they appear to do these things, it is an illusion that they can;
(c) there is a doubtful quality to their ability to do these things;
(d) a good photograph will always do these things;
(e) although they do, photographs ought not do these things.

4 Taking the whole passage into account, which of the following is *not* a *valid conclusion* from the writer's discussion of the photograph in the reporting of the funeral of David Foulkes?

(a) there is a different and more substantial way of looking at photographs possible to us;
(b) it is morally less problematic to look at photographs of the living than of the dead;
(c) it is possible for photographs to do more than give us immediacy of event;
(d) photography in newspapers raises difficult problems over how it is displayed;
(e) some photography may emotionally involve us in an important way.

2. MUSIC AND FORM

All art constantly aspires towards the condition of music. For while in all other kinds of art it is possible to distinguish the matter from the form, and the understanding can always make this distinction, yet it is the constant effort of art to obliterate it. That the mere matter of a poem, for instance, its subject, namely, its given incidents or situation - that the mere matter of a picture, the actual circumstances of an event, the actual topography of a landscape - should be nothing without the form, the spirit, of the handling, that this form, this mode of handling, should become an end in itself, should penetrate every part of the matter: this is what all art constantly strives after, and achieves in different degrees. . .

Art, then, is always striving to be independent of the mere intelligence, to become a matter of pure perception, to get rid of its responsibilities to its subject or material; the ideal examples of poetry and painting being those in which the constituent elements of the composition are so welded together, that the material or subject no longer strikes the intellect only; nor the form, the eye or the ear only; but form and matter, in their union or identity, present one single effect to the 'imaginative reason,' that complex faculty for which every thought and feeling is twin-born with its sensible analogue or symbol.

It is the art of music which most completely realises this artistic ideal, this perfect identification of matter and form. In its consummate moments, the end is not distinct from the means, the form from the matter, the subject from the expression; they inhere in and completely saturate each other; and to it, therefore, to the condition of its perfect moments, all the arts may be supposed constantly to tend and aspire. In music then, rather than poetry, is to be found the true type or measure of perfected art. Therefore, although each art has its incommunicable element, its untranslatable order of impressions, its unique mode of reaching the 'imaginative reason,' yet the arts may be represented as continually struggling after the law or principle of music, to a condition which music alone completely realises; and one of the chief functions of aesthetic criticism, dealing with the products of art, new or old, is to estimate the degree in which each of those products approaches, in this sense, to musical law.

1 Which of the following *best describes* the author's argument that music achieves an ideal relationship between matter and form?

(a) in music, there is no matter, but only form;
(b) in music, it is impossible to separate matter and form;
(c) in music, form is the predominant element, and matter is minimal;
(d) in music, neither matter nor form have to communicate anything;
(e) in music, there is no form, but only matter.

2 From the author's description, what is the 'imaginative reason'?

(a) the capacity to appreciate art;
(b) the capacity to imagine that art represents something else;
(c) the capacity to both experience and to make sense of our impressions;
(d) the capacity to create new thoughts and feelings;
(e) the capacity to imagine the ideal.

3 Which of the following is the *most relevant assumption* that the author makes in his argument that 'all art constantly aspires towards the condition of music'?

(a) it is in the nature of good art that the distinction between form and matter should be as minimal as possible;
(b) all arts share a common aesthetic criterion;
(c) all art intends to appeal to the 'imaginative reason';
(d) art criticism can accurately judge whether other art forms have achieved the condition of music;
(e) it is possible to identify what it is about 'musical law' that means it can serve as an artistic goal.

3. ASSISTED REPRODUCTION

The desire to have one's own biological children is, of course, nothing new. It has motivated human reproduction throughout the history of the species. What is new is both the ability and the inspiration for postmenopausal women to act on this desire. Moreover, the possibility of having a genetically related child is complemented by the inclination to experience pregnancy, both for one's own sense of self and to ensure the best possible foetal environment for one's offspring. This imperative to experience pregnancy has been extended to women past the age of menopause, thanks to the availability of assisted reproductive technologies. Contrary to the call of feminists in the 1970s to use technology to separate reproduction from the body - think of Shulamith Firestone's celebration of the potential of the artificial womb - biology and society have instead collaborated in establishing the importance of nature, namely, the mother's womb in foetal development. Technology is used not to replace, but to enhance nature, to allow for biologically 'natural' gestation.

Technology now also facilitates the use of one's own genetic material, so that there can be both a biological and a genetic connection to the child in spite of infertility. The recent innovation in the cryopreservation of oocytes affords young women today the opportunity to plan ahead for tomorrow, to have their own genetically related children on their own timetable. For women already past the age of menopause who did not freeze their eggs, they may resort to the use of a donor egg (another woman's genetic material) which can be fertilised by her male partner's sperm (and thus allowing for a genetic connection between father and child). Some prospective parents seeking to purchase eggs from donors who meet certain criteria have placed advertisements in college newspapers offering large sums of money (from $15,000 to $50,000) for women with certain physical and mental attributes. While height and eye colour are largely determined by genetics, the same cannot be said for creativity, athleticism, and high SAT scores. The effort to select a genotype based on the parents' phenotype harks back to the old eugenics of simplistic genetic determinism. If, however, the primacy of an individual's personal genes - the hallmark of the new eugenics - continues to hold sway, then we might expect to see more pregnancies using one's own frozen eggs rather than eggs donated by another.

This application of the new eugenics also comprises an element of the old eugenics in that access to assisted reproductive technologies for postmenopausal women is limited to those who can afford to pay for these medical services. In the United

States, only affluent women are able to take advantage of the choice to reproduce after menopause, unless Medicaid (and Medicare?) extends coverage to ART, which seems unlikely. Disparities in access to assisted reproductive technologies inversely mirror the differential use of reproductive control technologies. Put bluntly, low-income women are deterred from reproducing, while affluent women are encouraged to have children. For example, government policies in the 1990s strongly encouraged poor women to choose Norplant, the five-year contraceptive implant, over other methods of birth control. Medicaid covered the cost of Norplant insertion, and as a result, at least half of the women in America who used Norplant were Medicaid recipients. The pronatalist imperative to bear one's own genetically related children has been in large part restricted to the middle and upper classes - in effect, to the already economically well-born.

1 **Which of the following is *not* associated with the word 'technology'?**

(a) enhancement;
(b) opportunity;
(c) expense;
(d) equality;
(e) experience.

2 **What is the *significant point* that the author makes about prospective parents advertising to purchase eggs from donors?**

(a) parents seek children with similar qualities but different genes than themselves;
(b) parents seek children with different qualities but the same genes than themselves;
(c) parents seek ideal children;
(d) parents prefer mental qualities in children to physical qualities;
(e) parents seek the best qualified donors.

3 **What is the *similarity* that the writer sees in assisted reproduction technology between the 'old eugenics' and the 'new eugenics'?**

(a) there is an emphasis on preventing children;
(b) there is an emphasis on the poor having children;
(c) the emphasis to have or not to have children is placed on different people;
(d) there is a confusing mixed message about whether to have children;
(e) there is an emphasis on being sufficiently affluent to look after children.

4 **Which of the following is *implied but not stated* by the author's comment on the views of feminists of the 1970s?**

(a) they were opposed to reproduction by means of the mother's womb;
(b) they considered artificial reproduction to be superior;
(c) they believed that reproductive technology harmed women;
(d) they wished to achieve a new understanding of reproduction;
(e) they believed that reproduction could be stopped entirely.

4. COFFEE

Historians of stimulants have tried to invest coffee with characteristics that would explain its agreeability to the bourgeoisie. Coffee does not contain alcohol and can easily be promoted as an antidote, as a means to maintain energetic sobriety and keep working, a disposition in line with the ascetic ethos of the agents of early capitalism. There is no shortage of advertising material from the period to support such a view. Drawing on puritan coffee propaganda, the historian Wolfgang Schivelbusch asserts that, with coffee, rationalism entered the physiology of man. Its somatic effects associate it with the exhortation to constant alertness and activity.

However, to Habermas, the chemical constituents and invigorating effect of coffee do not play any overt role in the constitution of the public sphere. As a thinker with Marxist allegiances, he avoids the fetishism that seems to inhere in the genre of commodity histories, in which objects of consumption take on unexpected powers and become protagonists in adventurous narratives. Yet no Marxist would believe that social relations can be neatly disentangled from commodity capitalism. According to Habermas, bourgeois individuals are able to enter into novel kinds of relationships with one another in the coffeehouse because the links between family, civil society, and the state are restructured under capitalist conditions.

The capitalist reorganisation of the societal whole enables more fluid relations between individuals, whose social and economic ties predominantly assume contractual forms. The market economy allows agents of commerce to operate independently of societal bonds of lordship and servitude, but the household also ceases to be a site of manufacture and trade. As a consequence, the intimate familial circle of parents and children seems to be composed of autonomous individuals united not by production, but by mutual love and sympathy. Within the released sphere of intimacy, the bourgeoisie also discovers and explores a new mode of subjectivity, and the members of the family become readers and writers of emotionally saturated letters and diaries. On the basis of this new repertoire of experiences, they begin to conceive of themselves as human beings with an existence beyond prescribed official roles.

The private realm of human intimacy does not remain sealed off from other societal areas. Rather the individuals discourse with one another in new settings, such as the coffeehouse. When they do so, however, they retain their newfound status as autonomous and equal human beings, unburdened by the intricate feudal ceremonies through which rank was once ostentatiously displayed and corroborated. When the members of the bourgeoisie meet for coffee, they convene as participants in true humanity: they claim not to represent a particular consistency or interest, but to embody a universal community. In fact, it is partly by their claim to represent humanity as such rather than defined group within an established grid that they can arrogate to themselves jurisdiction over policy matters. Enlightened public opinion can legitimately check the exercise of political power, because in the public discourse that unfolds through the voluntary interaction among individuals unencumbered by feudal barriers, rational argument prevails over all other concerns.

1 In his discussion in the second paragraph, what does the writer think is *the most important thing* about coffee for *Habermas*?

(a) it is the novelty of coffee, and not its ingredients, that brings people together;
(b) people seem to like it more than anything else, hence its significance;
(c) coffee is inherently capitalist, hence it is controversial for Marxists;
(d) coffee is a social drink, and it is good that people drink it together in coffeehouses;
(e) coffee gives rise to coffeehouses, which under capitalism reorganises relationships.

2 Which of the following is *not* a valid contextual *interpretation* of the quotation from Schivelbusch that, 'with coffee, rationalism entered the physiology of man'?

(a) a certain philosophical view became a staple of daily life;
(b) the energy provided by coffee allowed people to take care of themselves better;
(c) the spirit of productivity began to inhere in commodities;
(d) the spirit of productivity became unavoidable in society;
(e) a certain moral view of life affected all aspects of a person's activity.

3 In the development that results in open public discourse, the writer presents *Habermas* as arguing for a *necessary* link between:

(a) the market economy and social autonomy;
(b) the market economy and coffee;
(c) the market economy and emotion;
(d) the market economy and intimacy;
(e) the market economy and family.

4 In the final paragraph, the writer explains Habermas' conclusion that 'Enlightened public opinion' can 'legitimately check the exercise of political power'. Which of the following *best describes* the reason that the writer presents *Habermas* as giving for that legitimacy?

(a) because when people come together, their arguments will be better than if they were isolated;
(b) because in voluntary and equal interaction, rationality prevails;
(c) because voluntary and equal participants have a claim to represent true humanity;
(d) because when the bourgeoisie come together, they are free from pressure or interest groups;
(e) because the intimacy of their universal community means they are more likely to be honest.

5. WAR

Almost every great nation has inherited certain questions, either with other nations or with sections of its own people, which it is quite impossible, in the present state of civilisation, to decide as matters between private individuals can be decided. During the last century at least half of the wars that have been fought have been civil and not foreign wars. There are big and powerful nations which habitually commit, either upon other nations or upon sections of their own people, wrongs so outrageous as to justify even the most peaceful persons in going to war. There are also weak nations so utterly incompetent either to protect the rights of foreigners against their own citizens, or to protect their own citizens against foreigners, that it becomes a matter of sheer duty for some outside power to interfere in connection with them. As yet in neither case is there any efficient method of getting international action; and if joint action by several powers is secured, the result is usually considerably worse than if only one Power interfered. The worst infamies of modern times—such affairs as the massacres of the Armenians by the Turks, for instance—have been perpetrated in a time of nominally profound international peace, when there has been a concert of big Powers to prevent the breaking of this peace, although only by breaking it could the outrages be stopped. Be it remembered that the peoples who suffered by these hideous massacres, who saw their women violated and their children tortured, were actually enjoying all the benefits of "disarmament". Otherwise they would not have been massacred; for if the Jews in Russia and the Armenians in Turkey had been armed, and had been efficient in the use of their arms, no mob would have meddled with them.

Yet amiable but fatuous persons, with all these facts before their eyes, pass resolutions demanding universal arbitration for everything, and the disarmament of the free civilized powers and their abandonment of their armed forces; or else they write well-meaning, solemn little books, or pamphlets or editorials, and articles in magazines or newspapers, to show that it is "an illusion" to believe that war ever pays, because it is expensive. This is precisely like arguing that we should disband the police and devote our sole attention to persuading criminals that it is "an illusion" to suppose that burglary, highway robbery and white slavery are profitable. It is almost useless to attempt to argue with these well-intentioned persons, because they are suffering under an obsession and are not open to reason. They go wrong at the outset, for they lay all the emphasis on peace and none at all on righteousness. They are not all of them physically timid men but they are usually men of soft life and they rarely possess a high sense of honour or a keen patriotism. They rarely try to prevent their fellow countrymen from insulting or wronging the people of other nations; but they always ardently advocate that we, in our turn, shall tamely submit to wrong and insult from other nations. As Americans their folly is peculiarly scandalous, because if the principles they now uphold are right, it means that it would have been better that Americans should never have achieved their independence, and better that, in 1861, they should have peacefully submitted to seeing their country split into half a dozen jangling confederacies and slavery made perpetual. If unwilling to learn from their own history, let those who think that it is an "illusion" to believe that a war ever benefits a nation look at the difference between China and Japan. China has neither a fleet nor an efficient army. It is a huge civilized empire, one of the most populous on the globe; and it has been the helpless prey of outsiders because it does not possess the power to fight. Japan stands on a footing of equality with European and American nations because it does possess this power. China now sees Japan, Russia, Germany, England and France in possession of fragments of her empire, and has twice within the lifetime of the present generation seen her capital in the hands of allied invaders, because she in very fact realises the ideals of the persons who wish the United States to disarm, and then trust that our helplessness will secure us a contemptuous immunity from attack by outside nations.

1 **In the first paragraph, the author argues:**

(a) that international action prevents atrocities;
(b) that international peace is best served by the joint action of big Powers;
(c) that we can never achieve international action;
(d) that action by a single Power is preferable to international action;
(e) that the idea of international action is of doubtful utility.

2 **What is the reason the author gives for the 'equality' between Japan and the other mentioned nations?**

(a) Japan has just as big an army as the other countries;
(b) civilised countries are equal, and Japan is a civilised country;
(c) Japan has the ability to fight;
(d) Japan has a naval power like the other countries;
(e) Japan has kept its territory intact.

3 **Which of the following pairs of ideas are *not* used as oppositions in the passage?**

(a) powerful countries and weak countries;
(b) citizens and foreigners;
(c) peace and righteousness;
(d) civil wars and foreign wars;
(e) right and duty.

4 **Which of the following adjectives is *not* used to convey approval in the passage?**

(a) well-intentioned;
(b) civilised;
(c) great;
(d) free;
(e) efficient.

6. THE ENGLISH MONARCHY

To state the matter shortly, royalty is a government in which the attention of the nation is concentrated on one person doing interesting actions. A Republic is a government in which that attention is divided between many, who are all doing uninteresting actions. Accordingly, so long as the human heart is strong and the human reason weak, royalty will be strong because it appeals to diffused feeling, and Republics weak because they appeal to the understanding. . .

The Queen is head of our society. If she did not exist the Prime Minister would be the first person in the country. He and his wife would have to receive foreign ministers, and occasionally foreign princes, to give the first parties in the country; he and she would be at the head of the pageant of life; they would represent England in the eyes of foreign nations; they would represent the Government of England in the eyes of the English.

It is very easy to imagine a world in which this change would not be a great evil. In a country where people did not care for the outward show of life, where the genius of the people was untheatrical, and they exclusively regarded the substance of things, this matter would be trifling. Whether Lord or Lady Derby received the foreign ministers, or Lord and Lady Palmerston, would be a matter of indifference; whether they gave the nicest parties would be important only to the persons at those parties. A nation of unimpressable philosophers would not care at all how the externals of life were managed. Who is the showman is not material unless you care about the show.

But of all nations in the world, the English are perhaps the least a nation of pure philosophers. It would be a very serious matter to us to change every four or five years the visible head of our world. We are not now remarkable for the highest sort of ambition; but we are remarkable for having a great deal of the lower sort of ambition and envy. The House of Commons is thronged with people who get there merely for 'social purposes,' as the phrase goes; that is, that they and their families may go to parties else impossible. Members of Parliament are envied by thousands merely for this frivolous glory, as a thinker calls it. If the highest post in conspicuous life were thrown open to public competition, this low sort of ambition and envy would be fearfully increased. Politics would offer a prize too dazzling for mankind; clever base people would strive for it, and stupid base people would envy it. Even now a dangerous distinction is given by what is exclusively called public life. The newspapers describe daily and incessantly a certain conspicuous existence; they comment on its characters, recount its details, investigate its motives, anticipate its course. They give a precedent and a dignity to that world which they do not give to any other. The literary world, the scientific world, the philosophical world, not only are not comparable in dignity to the political world, but in comparison are hardly worlds at all. The newspaper makes no mention of them, and could not mention them. As are the papers, so are the readers; they, by irresistible sequence and association, believe that those people who constantly figure in the papers are cleverer, abler, or at any rate, somehow higher, than other people. "I wrote books," we heard of a man saying, "for twenty years, and I was a nobody; I got into Parliament, and before I had taken my seat I had become somebody." English politicians are the men who fill the thoughts of the English public: they are the actors on the scene, and it is hard for the admiring spectators not to believe that the admired actor is greater than themselves. In this present age and country it would be very dangerous to give the slightest addition to a force already perilously great. If the highest social rank was to be scrambled for in the House of Commons, the number of social adventurers there would be incalculably more numerous, and infinitely more eager.

1 Which of the following is *not* meant by the author's expression 'the genius of the people'?

(a) the particular and distinctive qualities of the people;
(b) the notable feature that the people have in common;
(c) the prevalent views and attitudes of the people;
(d) the intelligence of the people;
(e) the character of the people.

2 What is the author's argument in favour of having a monarch as the head of state?

(a) a politician as head of state would be insufficiently theatrical;
(b) the people will be excessively captivated by a politician as head of state;
(c) having a monarch as head of state means that the position is not open to frivolous politicians;
(d) the number of politicians is already too great, and if the highest position was available, their numbers would increase;
(e) the people would experience too great a difficulty in adjusting to a change every four or five years.

3 When the author states that royalty is strong because it appeals to 'diffused feeling', which of the following comes closest to his meaning?

(a) royalty appeals to all people;
(b) royalty appeals to people's weaker emotions;
(c) royalty appeals to a wide range of people;
(d) royalty plays on ambiguous or uncertain feelings that people have;
(e) royalty appeals to many aspects of people's emotions.

4 From the information in the passage, which of the following *best describes* the relationship that the author sees between newspapers and public opinion?

(a) if newspapers attach great importance to certain people, then public opinion likewise regards them as important;
(b) public opinion is very interested in the activities of certain people, so newspapers reflect this interest:
(c) newspapers deliberately distort public opinion in favour of certain people;
(d) newspapers have no connection to public opinion;
(e) public opinion is merely low ambition and envy, and newspapers play upon this.

7. MODELS OF WELFARE STATES

Any system of social security and the provision of services draws an implicit demarcation line. This line divides categories of risks and contingencies that belong to a sphere that the respective individuals affected by such conditions can be expected to cope with by their means, on the one hand, from those categories of conditions that call for collective provisions, on the other. If I suffer from a common cold, I am, according to the logic of most welfare states and health systems, on this side of the line, as I am supposed to know what to do (and actually act upon that knowledge) in order to achieve a speedy recovery and to pay for whatever it costs to get there. In contrast, if I suffer from pneumonia, the remedial measures to be taken are typically specified by, provided for, and financed through public and other collective arrangements (insurance, licensed medical institutions, tax-subsidised occupational health plans, etc). In this way, welfare states can be looked at as sorting machines which assign deserts, rights, or legitimate needs-to-be-taken care of to categories of people in specified conditions, while leaving other conditions to the sphere of what is considered "normal": you have to cope with them by your own means, relying on markets and family support, or, failing that, simply accept them as unfortunate facts of life. Within welfare states and longitudinally, this demarcation line is never fixed and essentially contested. But cross-sectionally and between welfare states, the location of this divide differs greatly between individual states as well as types of welfare states.

The state socialist culture of social policy has located this moral demarcation line very far away from the extreme of market-mediated private provision and very close to the opposite extreme of the comprehensive caring state. The basic fact that there was, at least officially, no labour "market" but a pervasive system of administrative allocation of labour to jobs and status rights of jobholders was (rightly, for the duration of the system) seen as a blanket protection of the entire population from the risk of unemployment. Expectations of non-elites converged with the strategic orientation of the monopolistic ruling party in that benevolent state paternalism should govern most spheres of need (including, for instance, basic food, housing, education, vacation trips) of most categories of persons. Strategically, the institutions that were designed to embody and implement this set of social policy norms operated in the service of the objectives of keeping workers dependent, disciplined, and acquiescent, of rewarding loyalty towards the regime (as well as threatening sanctions for disloyalty), preventing "petit bourgeois individualism" and social differentiation among the worker-citizens, and of motivating work effort and productivity through the comprehensive guarantee of (job, income, housing, health, civic, etc) security. Services and benefits were allocated to a large extent at the point of production and through managerial discretion, rather than on the basis of individual rights that could be enforced in court. The system that provided security was distinctively "productivist," in that social rights of citizenship (as opposed to status rights of workers) played at best a marginal role. Collectivist and paternalist care privileged those preparing themselves for playing productive roles in schools and universities, those presently involved in the process of production, and the reproductive function of women (as well as in the process of the state's administering, policing, and protecting society from its "enemies"). People outside of (re)productive roles, mostly pensioners, were significantly worse off in terms of social protection. (The latter fact provides reason to caution against mistaking state socialist social policy for being based on "citizenship"; rather, effective citizenship was based upon the performance of the various "productive" roles just mentioned.)

1 In this passage, which of the following *best describes* the *difference* that the writer sees between 'social rights' and 'status rights'?

(a) status rights are not really rights, whereas social rights are;
(b) status rights cannot be enforced in court, whereas social rights can;
(c) status rights are only held by a few people, whereas social rights are for all;
(d) status rights pertain to facts about people, whereas social rights pertain to people generally;
(e) status rights disadvantage those with no status, whereas social rights advantage all.

2 In the first sentence of the passage, which of the following *best describes* the writer's *meaning* by stating that the demarcation line is 'implicit'?

(a) the line is always positioned arbitrarily;
(b) the line is always present, even if not articulated;
(c) the line is hidden from ordinary people;
(d) the position of the line is the subject of dispute and controversy;
(e) even if we cannot see the line, we can deduce its existence from evidence.

3 Which of the following is *not an accurate description* of the writer's discussion of having a common cold as opposed to having pneumonia to illustrate the logic of most welfare states?

(a) a paradigm;
(b) an example;
(c) a core case;
(d) a guide;
(e) a model.

8. INTERNET REGULATION

Where has the rational and balanced "netizen" gone, the well-behaved online citizen? The Internet seems to become an echo chamber for extreme opinions. Is Web 2.0 getting out of control? At first glance, the idea of the netizen is a mid-1990s response to the first wave of users that took over the Net. The netizen moderates, cools down heated debates, and above all responds in a friendly, non-repressive manner. The netizen does not represent the Law, is no authority, and acts like a personal advisor, a guide in a new universe. The netizen is thought to act in the spirit of good conduct and corporate citizenship. Users were to take social responsibility themselves — it was not a call for government regulation and was explicitly designed to keep legislators out of the Net. Until 1990, the late academic stage of the Net, it was presumed that all users knew the rules (also called netiquette) and would behave accordingly. (On Usenet there were no "netizens": everyone was a pervert.) Of course this was not always the case. When misbehaviour was noticed, the individual could be convinced to stop spamming, bullying, etc. This was no longer possible after 1995, when the Internet opened up to the general public. Because of the rapid growth of the World Wide Web, with the browsers that made it so much easier to use, the code of conduct developed over time by IT-engineers and scientists could no longer be passed on from one user to the next.

At the time, the Net was seen as a global medium that could not easily be controlled by national legislation. Perhaps there was some truth in this. Cyberspace was out of control, but in a nice and innocent way. That in a room next to the office of the Bavarian prime minister, the authorities had installed a task force to police the Bavarian part of the Internet, was an endearing and somewhat desperate image. At the time we had a good laugh about this predictably German measure.

9/11 and the dotcom crash cut the laughter short. Over a decade later, there are reams of legislation, entire governmental departments and a whole arsenal of software tools to oversee the National Web, as it is now called. Retrospectively, it is easy to dismiss the rational "netizen" approach as a libertarian *Gestalt*, a figure belonging to the neo-liberal age of deregulation. However the issues the netizen was invented to address have grown exponentially, not gone away. These days we would probably frame them as a part of education programs in schools and as general awareness campaigns. Identity theft is a serious business. Cyberbullying amongst children does happen and parents and teachers need to know how to identify and to respond to it. Much like the mid-1990s, we are still faced with the problem of "massification". The sheer number of users and the intensity with which people engage with the Internet is phenomenal. What perhaps has changed is that many no longer believe that the Internet community can sort out these issues itself. The Internet has penetrated society to such an extent that they have become one and the same.

1 What does the writer identify as the *main reason* for the shift from 'netizen' self-regulation to government regulation?

(a) governments realised that the internet could be easily controlled;
(b) governments decided that people could not be trusted to regulate themselves;
(c) too many people use the internet too intensely for it to be self-regulating;
(d) if governments regulate society, and the internet is now part of society, governments must now regulate the internet;
(e) internet dangers have grown to such an extent that it is no longer believed that self-regulation can effectively address them.

2 The writer states that 'the netizen does not represent the Law'. The writer compares the netizen to several other roles. Which of the following is the *best description* of the relationship the writer suggests between the netizen and those roles?

(a) they are analogous;
(b) they share a likeness;
(c) they are similar;
(d) they share a resemblance;
(e) they have an affinity.

3 Which of the following is *not* a valid contextual *interpretation* of the writer's comment that 'cyberspace was out of control, but in a nice and innocent way'?

(a) cyberspace is now out of control in a non-innocent way;
(b) cyberspace is now under control;
(c) cyberspace is now under control in a non-innocent way;
(d) cyberspace can never be controlled;
(e) cyberspace had few problems when it was this way.

9. INTEREST RATES

Mr. Locke, Mr. Law, and Mr. Montesquieu, as well as many other writers, seem to have imagined that the increase of the quantity of gold and silver, in consequence of the discovery of the Spanish West Indies, was the real cause of the lowering of the rate of interest through the greater part of Europe. Those metals, they say, having become of less value themselves, the use of any particular portion of them necessarily became of less value too, and consequently the price which could be paid for it. This notion, which at first sight seems so plausible, has been so fully exposed by Mr. Hume, that it is perhaps, unnecessary to say any thing more about it. The following very short and plain argument, however, may serve to explain more distinctly the fallacy which seems to have misled those gentlemen.

Before the discovery of the Spanish West Indies, 10 per cent seems to have been the common rate of interest through the greater part of Europe. It has since that time in different countries sunk to six, five, four and three per cent. Let us suppose that in every particular country the value of silver has sunk precisely in the same proportion as the rate of interest; and that in those countries, for example, where interest has been reduced from 10 to five per cent, the same quantity of silver can now purchase just half the quantity of goods which it could have purchased before. This supposition will not, I believe, be found anywhere agreeable to the truth; but it is the most favourable to the opinion which we are going to examine; and even upon this supposition it is utterly impossible that the lowering of the value of silver could have the smallest tendency to lower the rate of interest. If a hundred pounds are in those countries now of no more value than fifty pounds were then, 10 pounds must now be of no more value than five pounds were then. Whatever were the causes which lowered the value of the capital, the same must necessarily have lowered that of the interest, and exactly in the same proportion. The proportion between the value of the capital and that of the interest, must have remained the same, though the rate had never been altered. By altering the rate, on the contrary, the proportion between those two values is necessarily altered. If a hundred pounds now are worth no more than fifty were then, five pounds now can be worth no more than two pounds 10 shillings were then. By reducing the rate of interest, therefore, from 10 to five per cent, we give for the use of a capital, which is supposed to be equal to one-half of its former value, an interest which is equal to one-fourth only of the value of the former interest.

Any increase in the quantity of silver, while that of the commodities circulated by means of it remained the same, could have no other effect than to diminish the value of that metal. The nominal value of all sorts of goods would be greater, but their real value would be precisely the same as before. They would be exchanged for a greater number of pieces of silver; but the quantity of labour which they could command, the number of people whom they could maintain and employ, would be precisely the same. The capital of the country would be the same, though a greater number of pieces might be requisite for conveying any equal portion of it from one hand to another. The deeds of assignment, like the conveyances of a verbose attorney, would be more cumbersome, but the thing assigned would be precisely the same as before, and could produce only the same effects. The funds maintaining productive labour being the same, the demand for it would be the same. Its price or wages, therefore, though nominally greater, would really be the same. They would be paid in a greater number of pieces of silver; but they would purchase only the same quantity of goods. The profits of stock would be the same both nominally and really.

1   **The writer argues that:**

(a) lowering the value of capital lowers the rate of interest;
(b) increasing the value of capital increases the rate of interest;
(c) for a given interest rate, the value of capital is in direct proportion to the value of interest;
(d) altering interest rates results in the value of interest being out of proportion to the value of capital;
(e) increasing the amount of capital lowers the rate of interest.

2   **Which of the following is the *main flaw* that the author finds in the argument attributed to 'Mr Locke, Mr Law, and Mr Montesquieu'?**

(a) they are mistaken that there was an increase in the amount of capital;
(b) they are mistaken that increases in the amount of capital reduce its value;
(c) they are mistaken that rates of interest are relevant to the use of money;
(d) they are mistaken that increases in the amount of capital affects rates of interest;
(e) they are mistaken that portions of a quantity follow the same rules as the whole.

3   **Which of the following *best describes* the *difference* that the author sees in the passage between real value and nominal value?**

(a) nominal value is not properly a kind of value, whereas real value is;
(b) nominal value refers to the amount of money a thing can be exchanged for, whereas real value refers to the labour a thing can obtain;
(c) nominal value refers to prices, whereas real value refers to people;
(d) nominal value is changeable, whereas the real value of a thing is always constant;
(e) nominal value refers to goods, whereas real value refers to the services people provide.

4   **Which of the following *best describes* how the author *treats* the argument of 'Mr Locke, Mr Law, and Mr Montesquieu'?**

(a) the author takes their argument at its strongest;
(b) the author misrepresents their argument;
(c) the author does not understand their argument;
(d) the author explains their argument badly;
(e) the author takes their argument at its weakest.

10. PRAGUE AND KAFKA

Of all the symbols of this repressed Czech-German-Jewish history, the most memorable is the asylum for mentally damaged war-wounded, founded largely by Kafka himself in 1916-7 and still extant more or less as he left it, in a place which was, in Kafka's day, rather wonderfully called Frankenstein. Now, you would imagine, would you not, that Dr Kafka's Asylum for Mentally Damaged Soldiers in Frankenstein would be an irresistible magnet for young film-makers? In fact, it is entirely unknown to the tourist trade and scarcely more known to scholars, despite its being the one actual relic of Kafka's life that would truly support his quasi-saintly image. When I went there last year with the BBC, the doctors had no idea of the Kafka connection at all and told us we were the first film crew ever to visit — this despite its being scarcely two hours drive from any of the mighty universities of Munich, Dresden, and Leipzig, never mind only an hour from Prague.

Why is the place so ignored? I think the answer is simple: because this was a German-speaking area until 1945, and Kafka's mental hospital was (by his own express avowal) founded exclusively for German-speaking soldiers. The good soldier Schweyk, however shell-shocked, would simply not have made Kafka's linguistic cut.

All this is perfectly well known about but never spoken of, either by tourist guides or literary hagiographers. The fact of the truth about Kafka makes it seem, on some dreary, sunless level athwart the glooming flats where psychology and culture interweave ineluctably, vaguely proper, if endlessly sad, that Prague has become what it is: a place of booze, brothels and endless tourist shops selling babushka dolls to overnight trippers unable to distinguish between Czech and Russian culture. The facts will be efficiently repressed in the name of business, locked away in some lumber-room of the mind, like Josef K.'s sado-masochistic vision in *The Trial*, wiped clean by the kerosene wake of the Ryanair flight home. Maybe, when your history is as damaged as Prague's, repression is a necessary part of survival (Freud never said it wasn't: he only said that if repression starts to cause neurosis, it is best identified). Certain demonstrable facts — that the photogenic city is really German, that in Kafka's day the German-speaking police and army repeatedly broke up Czech anti-Jewish riots — are simply no good at all in a place that must look to the future because the past is so tortured.

There remains the question that rears up — vengefully unrepressed at last! — after Gregor Samsa's metamorphosis into a giant bug (the story is a black comedy, by the way, whose nearest ancestor is very clearly Dostoyevsky's wonderful "The

Double"): "but what [thinks the giant bug!] if all this peace, this prosperity, this contentment, should now come to a terrible end?" Over the last decade, Prague has located its salvation in America, the friendly Hegemon that is always ready to treat history as bunk, the Empire which, in the days of its triumphs, never occupied a country, only minds. But the Imperium of the Second Chance visibly ebbs, its mental hold on the world bankrupted, its universal dream of freedom without frontiers shrunk tragically into futile little wars over nastily real, past-haunted desert acres. Meanwhile the Tzardom, replete with energy, revives from the dead, red-shoulder boards and all; Western Europe, that oft-raped widow, dithers and bickers; and Germany (of whose economy the Czech is in practice virtually a satellite), no longer quite the Swiss-clean, Rhine-centred, self-effacing country of recent memory, finds its attention shifting to those lands of cheap gas, low wages and faded Habsburg town halls which were always Berlin's natural sphere of concern.

1 **Which of the following is a *fact* rather than the writer's *opinion*?**

(a) 'the most memorable is the asylum for mentally-damaged war-wounded';
(b) 'the facts will be efficiently repressed in the name of business';
(c) 'repression is a necessary part of survival';
(d) 'Josef K.'s sado-masochistic vision in *The Trial*';
(e) 'those lands of cheap gas, low wages and faded Habsburg town halls which were always Berlin's natural sphere of concern'.

2 **In which of the following is the writer *not* using heavy *sarcasm*?**

(a) 'wiped clean by the kerosene wake of the Ryanair flight home';
(b) 'on some dreary, sunless level athwart the glooming flats where psychology and culture interweave ineluctably';
(c) 'the Empire which, in the days of its triumphs, never occupied a country, only minds';
(d) 'no longer quite the Swiss-clean, Rhine-centered, self-effacing country of recent memory';
(e) 'endless tourist shops selling babushka dolls to overnight trippers unable to distinguish between Czech and Russian culture'.

3 **From the *whole* of the passage, which of the following do you think *best* describes the reason why the writer claims that it is 'vaguely proper, if endlessly sad, that Prague has become what it is'?**

(a) Prague has always been divided and unsure of its identity;
(b) no one has taken any interest in Prague, so it has become neglected;
(c) Prague has never known what to make of its history;
(d) Prague has historically always been a hotspot for tourists;
(e) Kafka himself could not distinguish between Czech and Russian culture.

11. CHILD PSYCHOLOGY

Without the intention of making a comprehensive study of these phenomena I availed myself of an opportunity which offered of elucidating the first game invented by himself of a boy eighteen months old. It was more than a casual observation, for I lived for some weeks under the same roof as the child and his parents, and it was a considerable time before the meaning of his puzzling and continually repeated performance became clear to me.

The child was in no respect forward in his intellectual development; at eighteen months he spoke only a few intelligible words, making besides sundry significant sounds which were understood by those about him. But he made himself understood by his parents and the maid-servant, and had a good reputation for behaving 'properly'. He did not disturb his parents at night; he scrupulously obeyed orders about not touching various objects and not going into certain rooms; and above all he never cried when his mother went out and left him for hours together, although the tie to his mother was a very close one: she had not only nourished him herself, but had cared for him and brought him up without any outside help. Occasionally, however, this well-behaved child evinced the troublesome habit of flinging into the corner of the room or under the bed all the little things he could lay his hands on, so that to gather up his toys was often no light task. He accompanied this by an expression of interest and gratification, emitting a loud long-drawn-out 'o-o-o-oh' which in the judgement of the mother (one that coincided with my own) was not an interjection but meant 'go away' *(fort)*. I saw at last that this was a game, and that the child used all his toys only to play 'being gone' *(fortsein)* with them. One day I made an observation that confirmed my view. The child had a wooden reel with a piece of string wound round it. It never occurred to him, for example, to drag this after him on the floor and so play horse and cart with it, but he kept throwing it with considerable skill, held by the string, over the side of his little draped cot, so that the reel disappeared into it, then said his significant 'o-o-o-oh' and drew the reel by the string out of the cot again, greeting its reappearance with a joyful *'Da'* (there). This was therefore the complete game, disappearance and return, the first act being the only one generally observed by the onlookers, and the one untiringly repeated by the child as a game for its own sake, although the greater pleasure unquestionably attached to the second act.

The meaning of the game was then not far to seek. It was connected with the child's remarkable cultural achievement—the foregoing of the satisfaction of an instinct—as the result of which he could let his mother go away without making any fuss. He made it right with himself, so to speak, by dramatising the same disappearance and return with the objects he had at hand. It is of course of no importance for the affective value of this game whether the child invented it himself or adopted it from a suggestion from outside. Our interest will attach itself to another point. The departure of the mother cannot possibly have been pleasant for the child, nor merely a matter of indifference. How then does it accord with the pleasure-principle that he repeats this painful experience as a game? The answer will perhaps be forthcoming that the departure must be played as the necessary prelude to the joyful return, and that in this latter lay the true purpose of the game. As against this, however, there is the observation that the first act, the going away, was played by itself as a game and far more frequently than the whole drama with its joyful conclusion.

1 **What does the author identify as the *main cause* of the game the child is playing?**

(a) the child is lonely, and needs to amuse himself;
(b) the child finds his mother's absence inexplicable, and needs to repeat it;
(c) the child is glad that his mother is gone, and is celebrating;
(d) the child is trying to cope with his mother's absence by repeating it;
(e) the child thinks that by pulling back the string, he makes his mother return.

2 **Which of the following *comes closest* to explaining why the author thinks that it is 'of no importance for the affective value of this game whether the child invented it himself or adopted it from a suggestion from outside'?**

(a) the reason the child is playing the game would be the same in any case;
(b) because the only people who could suggest the game were those close to him, it is still emotional;
(c) if the child were very original, it would mean his experience was not typical;
(d) all children play games, and the games are significant in themselves;
(e) in psychology, where ideas come from is never relevant.

3 **In their context in the passage, which of the following phrases does *not* introduce a new argument?**

(a) 'as against this. . .';
(b) 'it was connected with. . .';
(c) 'the answer. . .';
(d) 'I saw at last. . .';
(e) 'the meaning. . .'.

12. EIGHTEENTH CENTURY MANNERS

I make a difference between good manners and good breeding; although, in order to vary my expression, I am sometimes forced to confound them. By the first, I only understand the art of remembering and applying certain settled forms of general behaviour. But good breeding is of a much larger extent; for besides an uncommon degree of literature sufficient to qualify a gentleman for reading a play, or a political pamphlet, it takes in a great compass of knowledge; no less than that of dancing, fighting, gaming, making the circle of Italy, riding the great horse, and speaking French; not to mention some other secondary, or subaltern accomplishments, which are more easily acquired. So that the difference between good breeding and good manners lies in this, that the former cannot be attained to by the best understandings, without study and labour; whereas a tolerable degree of reason will instruct us in every part of good manners, without other assistance.

I can think of nothing more useful upon this subject, than to point out some particulars, wherein the very essentials of good manners are concerned, the neglect or perverting of which doth very much disturb the good commerce of the world, by introducing a traffic of mutual uneasiness in most companies.

First, a necessary part of good manners, is a punctual observance of time at our own dwellings, or those of others, or at third places; whether upon matter of civility, business, or diversion; which rule, though it be a plain dictate of common reason, yet the greatest minister I ever knew was the greatest trespasser against it; by which all his business doubled upon him, and placed him in a continual arrear. Upon which I often used to rally him, as deficient in point of good manners. I have known more than one ambassador, and secretary of state with a very moderate portion of intellectuals, execute their offices with good success and applause, by the mere force of exactness and regularity. If you duly observe time for the service of another, it doubles the obligation; if upon your own account, it would be manifest folly, as well as ingratitude, to neglect it. If both are concerned, to make your equal or inferior attend on you, to his own disadvantage, is pride and injustice.

Ignorance of forms cannot properly be styled ill manners; because forms are subject to frequent changes; and consequently, being not founded upon reason, are beneath a wise man's regard. Besides, they vary in every country; and after a short period of time, very frequently in the same; so that a man who travels, must needs be at first a stranger to them in every court through which he passes; and perhaps at his return, as much a stranger in his own; and after all, they are easier to be remembered or forgotten than faces or names.

Indeed, among the many impertinences that superficial young men bring with them from abroad, this bigotry of forms is one of the principal, and more prominent than the rest; who look upon them not only as if they were matters capable of admitting of choice, but even as points of importance; and are therefore zealous on all occasions to introduce and propagate the new forms and fashions they have brought back with them. So that, usually speaking, the worst bred person in the company is a young traveller just returned from abroad.

1 Which of the following is *implied but not stated* in the author's discussion of 'forms'?

(a) knowledge of forms cannot be taught, because forms are irrational;
(b) any subject that changes very frequently is not worth studying;
(c) people can only be blamed for being unaware of rational things;
(d) the best things to study are rational things;
(e) only foolish people bother to study forms.

2 The author uses the word 'bigotry' to mean:

(a) ignorance;
(b) overestimation;
(c) hatred;
(d) flattery;
(e) boredom.

3 Using the whole passage and applying the author's definition, which of the following is *not* a difference between good manners and good breeding?

(a) it takes more intelligence to be well bred than it does to be well mannered;
(b) punctuality is essential to good manners, whereas it is not essential for good breeding;
(c) good breeding is about ourselves, whereas good manners is about how we behave to others;
(d) good manners comprises common sense behaviour, whereas good breeding need not;
(e) good breeding takes real effort, whereas good manners can be attained quite easily.

PART II:
ESSAY QUESTIONS

PRACTICE TEST INSTRUCTIONS

This section has **five** essay questions.

You should select and answer **one** question in Part II (Section B).

Time allowed: 40 minutes

1 Make the best case for charging undergraduate university students the full cost of their degrees.

2 What is equality and why does it matter?

3 'The banning of outward religious symbols such as wearing the burkha or the Cross exemplifies Western society's inability to cope with cultural and social diversity.' Do you agree?

4 Critically examine the reasons for and against introducing proportional representation in the UK.

5 'In light of the recent financial crisis, the UK has nothing to lose by adopting the euro.' Discuss.

PART I:
MULTIPLE CHOICE ANSWERS AND GUIDANCE

1. NEWSPAPERS AND PHOTOGRAPHY

1 In the first paragraph, by claiming that newspapers showed a lack of 'reflexivity', the writer is:

The correct answer is (c). The question is asking you to identify the **argument** the author is making. You are guided to a specific part of the passage, so it is important that you think carefully about the argument of the whole paragraph. Only (c) is in fact the point that the author makes.

2 In the second paragraph, what is the *significance* that the writer sees in the 'more reflective' position of newspapers as opposed to other media?

The correct answer is (d). Here, the question is asking you to identify a specific point that the author is making within the context of the argument of the whole passage. You must relate this specific point to the wider argument, and often this specific point will be an intermediate stage in that argument. It is important that you look closely at what you are being asked, and do not introduce elements which only occur later in the passage. The author at this stage is making quite a modest point which prepares the ground for later analysis. Before answering, look again at the structure of the passage, and appreciate where the part you are guided to occurs in the structure of the whole argument. This will help you isolate the precise point the author makes.

3 When the writer claims that photographs may be used as *'seemingly* transparent windows onto the world', which may turn those looking at the pictures into *'apparent* witnesses of places and people', what is the point that the writer makes by using these qualifiers?

The correct answer is (c). The question is inviting you to examine the **effect** that the author wishes to achieve by using particular language. In these questions, you should not rely on your independent understanding of the meaning of these words, but rather analyse what function they are playing in the sentences in which they occur. This might be completely different from their ordinary meaning, especially if the author is using them in an ironic or sarcastic sense. Here, the tone of the sentence in which the words are found is muted and does not make any of the stronger claims contained in (a), (b), (d) or (e). Therefore (c) is the answer consistent with the effect of uncertainty and doubt about the qualities attributed that the author achieves.

4 Taking the whole passage into account, which of the following is *not* a *valid conclusion* from the writer's discussion of the photograph in the reporting of the funeral of David Foulkes?

The correct answer is (b). The question is testing your ability to draw logical conclusions from the passage. Often, many modest claims can be concluded from a passage but very few 'strong' or essential claims; in an argumentative passage, there will generally just be one strong conclusion, which is the one the author argues for. Once you have read through and understood the argument that an author is making, this will allow you to appreciate whether certain of the multiple choice options go beyond anything the author has said. This is the case here: (b) is a very strong claim which the author does not make and which cannot be concluded from the argument. All of the other options are weaker claims which are genuine (if rather dull) conclusions from the argument.

2. MUSIC AND FORM

1 Which of the following *best describes* the author's argument that music achieves an ideal relationship between matter and form?

The correct answer is (b). This is an argument identification question which requires you to select the option which corresponds most closely with the argument the author makes in the passage. A close reading of the passage should mean that you were able to **distinguish** the parts of the author's argument in which he considers the relationship of art in general to matter and form from those parts (most explicitly in the third paragraph) where he relates these ideas to music and its 'perfect identification of matter and form'.

2 From the author's description, what is the 'imaginative reason'?

The correct answer is (c). This is a difficult question since you have only one sentence of the author's from which to construct his definition: 'that complex faculty for which every thought and feeling is twin-born with its sensible analogue or symbol'. The most productive way of reaching the correct answer is to break down this sentence into its constituent parts. The author talks about **both** thoughts and feelings, on the one hand, **and** their 'sensible' analogue or symbol, on the other. He is trying to convey the idea that the imaginative reason is concerned with making sense of the thoughts and feelings which our perceptions and experience of art produce in us. Hopefully, the reference to 'symbols' in the definition will not have led you to select option (b).

3 Which of the following is the *most relevant assumption* that the author makes in his argument that 'all art constantly aspires towards the condition of music'?

The correct answer is (a). There are many possible assumptions which might be behind the author's argument in this passage. The question specifically asks you however to identify the most relevant assumption to the particular argument that the author makes about art aspiring to the condition of music. The detailed discussion in the first paragraph that art in general strives to obliterate the distinction between form and matter is the preparation to his more specific argument about music. Nowhere is it questioned that it might not necessarily be in the nature of good art to obliterate this distinction; option (a) is therefore the unspoken assumption which underlies the author's argument.

3. ASSISTED REPRODUCTION

1 — Which of the following is *not* associated with the word 'technology'?

The correct answer is (d). This question requires you to have digested the whole passage first, and then to have read through it again, looking closely at the usage in context of the particular word specified in the question. It is important to appreciate that 'association' is not simply a matter of looking at the other words appearing adjacent in the passage to the specified word. It also encompasses tone and an appreciation of the stage of the argument the author has reached. Here, finding the answer is straightforward: the author explicitly makes the point that there is a certain inequality surrounding the actual usage of assisted reproduction technology. Inverting this statement allows you to find a word, 'equality', which is **not** associated with the word 'technology'.

2 — What is the *significant point* that the author makes about prospective parents advertising to purchase eggs from donors?

The correct answer is (a). This question targets your sense of relevance. The author makes many arguments in this passage, and this question picks up on your ability to separate out the significant from the incidental. This can only be done by measuring individual arguments against the overall argument made in the passage. You are guided to a specific part of the author's argument in your instruction to examine the treatment of prospective parents advertising to purchase eggs from donors, and must identify the significant point the author makes. Here, the overall argument against which you will determine relevance is the author's discussion throughout of the similarities to, and differences from, the 'old eugenics' that the 'new eugenics' exhibits. This is an aspect of similarity, as you should have picked up from the author's discussion of 'selecting a genotype based on the parents' phenotype'.

3 — What is the *similarity* that the writer sees in assisted reproduction technology between the 'old eugenics' and the 'new eugenics'?

The correct answer is (c). This question draws on the same skills as the question above, but is distinct in that it asks you to concentrate on the main argument and identify the **explicit** similarity that the author sees. This is therefore an argument identification question.

4	**Which of the following is *implied but not stated* by the author's comment on the views of feminists of the 1970s?**

The correct answer is (d). Hopefully, you will have recognised that this is an interpretation question in the sense that was discussed in Chapter 5. The two-step inquiry that we discussed will be helpful once again in reaching the correct answer. First, what is the argument that is explicitly being made? Second, thinking in terms of consistency, of the options given by the question which, though not stated in so many words, is consistent with the text the question refers you to? The key in this question is distinguishing between the two strands of argument the author makes in the first paragraph. The author is *contrasting* the position of 1970s feminists with what is identified as the current prevailing position. Once you have appreciated this, it should be easier to arrive at the correct implication from the contrast to the feminist view. Options (b), (c), and (e) are not sufficiently closely related to the argument the author makes. Option (a), though closely related, is much too strong a claim from the information presented in the passage. Only (d) is both sufficiently close to the author's explicit discussion and a reasonable implication from the information presented.

4. COFFEE

1 In his discussion in the second paragraph, what does the writer think is *the most important thing* about coffee for *Habermas?*

The correct answer is (e). The question is testing your ability to separate out the author's own argument from another person's argument which the author is reporting. Once this is appreciated, the question then becomes a case of identifying the argument that is made from close attention to that reporting by the author.

2 Which of the following is *not* a valid contextual *interpretation* of the quotation from Schivelbusch that, 'with coffee, rationalism entered the physiology of man'?

The correct answer is (b). The question is testing your ability to appreciate the point that the author makes by citing another writer. This is a short quotation in a specific context, but it is not in itself detailed enough to allow a definitive interpretation to be made. The question tests thus **both** your appreciation of the effect of quotation **and** your understanding of the argument. You must therefore test the interpretations given against the **context** of the section of the passage you are guided to. All of the options given are potential contextual interpretations except (b).

3 In the development that results in open public discourse, the writer presents *Habermas* as arguing for a *necessary* link between:

The correct answer is (a). The question tests your ability to understand the **parts** of the author's argument. The LNAT will often require you to identify **necessary links** in the argument contained in a passage. This involves not only a comprehension of the argument, but an understanding of its structure. What does the passage indicate that the development of the market economy necessarily involves? Only (a) is given as essential and necessary in the passage.

4 In the final paragraph, the writer explains Habermas' conclusion that 'Enlightened public opinion' can 'legitimately check the exercise of political power'. Which of the following *best describes* the reason that the writer presents *Habermas* as giving for that legitimacy?

The correct answer is (b). This question tests your comprehension of the writer's reporting of the views of Habermas in the final paragraph. It is important to read the question carefully and make sure that you match the justification to the conclusion that you are being asked to consider; when the views of another writer are reported, often different elements are mixed in to a single part of the passage. For example, several of the options play upon Habermas' emphasis on 'voluntary and equal' participants - it would be easy to confuse the justification for the legitimacy the question asks you by citing the universal humanity explanation that Habermas gives, and thus choosing (c). Close attention to the context of the passage and to the question you are being asked will allow you to select the right answer.

5. WAR

1	In the first paragraph, the author argues:

The correct answer is (e). The key to this question is remaining focused on what the author actually says, as distinct from what the author almost says or appears to say. Option (e) is the best expression of the author's point.

2	What is the reason the author gives for the 'equality' between Japan and the other mentioned nations?

The correct answer is (c). Once again, this question tests your ability to identify arguments made, with the added difficulty of those arguments appearing within what is a generally discursive and conversational passage. In amidst the **discussion** the author has on this point - the contrast between Japan and China as a specific example of his argument about armament - a number of elements are mentioned, such as naval power, which are not developed further. The core of the point is simply the argument at its most explicit: (c).

3	Which of the following pairs of ideas are *not* used as oppositions in the passage?

The correct answer is (e). This question is asking you to think carefully about how words are used in the passage. It is again a mistake to rely on your extra-textual understanding of the meaning of these words to answer the question, because in many texts this will not lead you to the correct answer. In this passage, 'peace' and 'righteousness', though they are discussed disjunctively, nevertheless are not used as oppositions. The writer does not present them as contrasting ideas. The argument the writer makes complains of an *imbalance* in emphasis between them, but that is not the same. Again, (e) is the correct answer **not because** 'peace' and 'righteousness' are not in their nature opposing concepts, but because the author does not **use them** as opposing ideas.

4	Which of the following adjectives is *not* used to convey approval in the passage?

The correct answer is (a). Similarly, this question concerns how individual words are used by the author in the passage. This question illustrates starkly our point about the perils of relying on your extra-textual understanding of the meaning of words. 'Well-intentioned' is used with a pejorative overtone in this passage. The author uses it with the suggestion of pompousness or self-righteousness. A great deal can be understood about particular points that authors make by paying close attention to otherwise positive words which are used with varying degrees of negative meaning, and the LNAT rewards your ability to recognise this.

6. THE ENGLISH MONARCHY

1 Which of the following is *not* meant by the author's expression 'the genius of the people'?

The correct answer is (d). All of the sentences in which the author uses this expression are concerned to show that the English have a certain quality or attitude or perception - in this case, theatricality or showiness. The question is concerned to test that you are analysing the meaning of a word which you are guided to in terms of its function in the passage, rather than on the basis of your independent understanding of its meaning. In this case, the more common, independent meaning of the word 'genius' would have given you the incorrect answer.

2 What is the author's argument in favour of having a monarch as the head of state?

The correct answer is (c). Hopefully this should have been relatively clear to you on a careful reading of the long final paragraph of the passage. If you were tempted to choose (e), it is important to note that the question asks you to identify the **argument** that the author makes in favour of having a monarch as the head of state. The author's comment that it would be a serious matter to the English to have to change every four or five years is an observation which serves to preface his argument, which is found later.

3 When the author states that royalty is strong because it appeals to 'diffused feeling', which of the following comes closest to his meaning?

The correct answer is (e). This is a complex question since on first sight, several of the options are plausible. A close reading of the context should have made clear to you that the writer is talking about wide or spread out appeal, rather than weak appeal, meaning that you can discount options (b) and (d). Further, the writer is clearly not making so strong a claim that royalty appeals to all people, so (a) is inapplicable. It is however equally plausible to think that by 'diffuse' the author means either a wide range of feelings, or a wide range of people, either (c) or (e). What should have convinced you in favour of (e) is the contrast the writer makes in the same sentence; the writer **opposes** the appeal of diffuse feeling with appeal to the understanding, making clear that with diffuse feeling he is talking about emotions rather than the number of people affected.

4 From the information in the passage, which of the following *best describes* the relationship that the author sees between newspapers and public opinion?

The correct answer is (a). The author makes an explicit statement that 'as are the papers, so are the readers', so whatever else the author may have meant, he clearly gives strong indication that he thinks along the lines suggested by (a).

7. MODELS OF WELFARE STATES

---

1 In this passage, which of the following *best describes* the *difference* that the writer sees between 'social rights' and 'status rights'?

The correct answer is (d). The question is asking you which of the answers is the best expression of an element of the author's argument which is not central, yet to which the author clearly and explicitly refers. The passage sets up an opposition between these two concepts. From the points in the passage which do bear on this, what is the **essential** difference actually made? None of the answers are explicitly mentioned, yet some come close. The question is thus asking you to make a judgement on relevance measured against the comments in the passage. Only (d) is consistent with all the references that the author makes.

---

2 In the first sentence of the passage, which of the following *best describes* the writer's *meaning* by stating that the demarcation line is 'implicit'?

The correct answer is (b). You are guided to a specific sentence, and the question is asking you to make a conclusion from the context of that sentence. It is crucial therefore that you do not introduce elements which - however valid - are outside of that context. All of the other answers are outside the context to which the question refers you; only (b) is contained within it. Finding the correct answer requires you to think carefully about the **language** in the sentence and the **argument** which immediately surrounds it.

---

3 Which of the following is *not an accurate description* of the writer's discussion of having a common cold as opposed to having pneumonia to illustrate the logic of most welfare states?

The correct answer is (a). The LNAT will indirectly test your understanding of words outside the passage when asking you to make a judgement about words within the passage. Which of these words which the author does **not** use is correctly applied to this feature of the passage? Here, the question is asking the reverse: all of the following are correctly applied to the part of the passage mentioned, except one. Finding out which one is applied wrongly requires you to have an understanding of the meaning of these words. (b) through (e) are all broad and good descriptions of the writer's discussion, but (a) should stand out to you as a more specialised term with a specific meaning not relevant here.

8. INTERNET REGULATION

1 What does the writer identify as the *main reason* for the shift from 'netizen' self-regulation to government regulation?

The correct answer is (e). It is important to keep clear that you are being asked to identify the **main reason**, and not just any reason which the writer might indeed provide in the passage. This is relevant here in that either (c) or (d) might have appeared to you to have been the correct answer, but the question asks you about the shift from the netizen to the new model in the context of *regulation*. The writer explicitly relates the netizen to the idea of regulation. It is stated that 'the issues the netizen was invented to address have grown exponentially, not gone away'. The author expands upon this theme when illustrating the transition, and (c) is introduced as a subordinate point to (e).

2 The writer states that 'the netizen does not represent the Law'. The writer compares the netizen to several other roles. Which of the following is the *best description* of the relationship the writer suggests between the netizen and those roles?

The correct answer is (a). This is a question which *appears* to very directly test your understanding both of the nature of the author's comparison and of the meaning of the options presented to you. The differences between the options - though real - are extremely subtle. However, close attention to the question should quickly reveal to you that you are not in fact required to know the difference between concepts sharing an affinity and concepts sharing a resemblance. You are in fact only required to recognise that the author is making an *analogy* between the netizen and the other roles which the author mentions, therefore (a) is the correct answer. The question tests only your ability to detect the device of analogy. This question is a good illustration of the advantages of positive reasoning over negative reasoning. It would be extremely time-consuming for you to work through the options and strike out those which are not appropriate based on the shades of meaning between them; that is, to reason negatively. Quickly identifying what the question requires of you and selecting the most appropriate answer (reasoning positively) will be rewarded by the LNAT.

3 Which of the following is *not* a valid contextual *interpretation* of the writer's comment that 'cyberspace was out of control, but in a nice and innocent way'?

The correct answer is (d). This question requires you to isolate which of the options is an invalid interpretation of the quoted statement in the context of the passage. It should hopefully be clear to you that option (d) is a claim which goes beyond anything stated by the author, and is therefore far too strong a claim to be a valid contextual interpretation of the quoted statement.

9. INTEREST RATES

1	**The writer argues that:**

The correct answer is (c). This is an argument identification question. This is a difficult passage, and to correctly identify the argument made by the author (as distinct from the argument he is controverting) you must pay very careful attention to the parts of the passage where the author sets out his argument, rather than prepares the ground for argument. Here, the particular skill being tested is your ability to distinguish **the argument** made from **examples** or **instances** of that argument. Option (c) is the argument made by the author.

2	**Which of the following is the *main flaw* that the author finds in the argument attributed to 'Mr Locke, Mr Law, and Mr Montesquieu'?**

The correct answer is (d). This question tests your ability to detect where the author is examining the argument of others as distinct from advancing fresh views. Here, the author's disagreement with the other writers quoted is used to build the argument advanced in the passage, and the question challenges you to isolate the author's argument at the stage where the focus of the passage is still on the views of the other writers. Look carefully at the stages by which the argument proceeds, and ask yourself - given that you know from the first paragraph the argument the author wishes to convince the reader of - what is the main point of disagreement between the author and the other writers?

3	**Which of the following *best describes* the *difference* that the author sees in the passage between real value and nominal value?**

The correct answer is (b). This is an argument characterisation question, but it sticks closely to the wording of the passage, given that this is a complex and technical point. Nevertheless, close attention to the passage should allow you to arrive at the correct answer by understanding the opposition the author sets up. After introducing the terms 'nominal' and 'real' value, in the next sentence the author, without repeating the terms, *rephrases* the **same** point: 'they would be exchanged for a greater number of pieces of silver, but the quantity of labour which they could command, the number of people whom they could maintain and employ would be precisely the same'.

4	**Which of the following *best describes* how the author *treats* the argument of 'Mr Locke, Mr Law, and Mr Montesquieu'?**

The correct answer is (a). Hopefully it should be clear to you that the author is using an argumentative device. The author is taking the quoted writers' argument at its strongest, that is, the author is accepting for the time being premises which the argument advanced in the passage need not accept, in order to show the weakness of their logic. Once you have identified the overall structure of the *author's* argument, you should be able to arrive straightforwardly at the correct answer.

10. PRAGUE AND KAFKA

1 Which of the following is a *fact* rather than the writer's *opinion*?

The correct answer is (d). The question is asking you to **interpret** from the **tone** of the passage the difference between fact and opinion. This is difficult in this passage because the tone is extremely critical throughout. However, the answer in this case is clear from careful attention to the context in which each comment is made: (a), (b), (c) and (e) are all statements which carry the writer's point of view forward, and are topics about which multiple views might be held. However, (d) is a reference to part of what happens in a work of literature - made clear by the author's acknowledgement of the source and italicisation of the title. It is a fact that (d) is contained in the work of literature, and the tone of reporting that the author uses here is distinct from his tone when discussing the matters in the rest of the passage.

2 In which of the following is the writer *not* using heavy *sarcasm*?

The correct answer is (c). The question is asking you to **analyse** the **tone** that the writer uses in each of the given statements in their context. It is impossible to make this judgement by analysing the statements as they are listed in the question. You must look carefully at precisely in which sentence they are contained, and ask yourself whether the given quality - in this case, sarcasm - is present. The tone of (c) is distinctly different from sarcasm. It is gentler than the other comments, and its tone is better described as nostalgic or wistful.

3 From the *whole* of the passage, which of the following do you think *best describes* the reason why the writer claims that it is 'vaguely proper, if endlessly sad, that Prague has become what it is'?

The correct answer is (a). The question tests your ability to digest the **whole** of a very diverse passage and identify which of the possible reasons the author himself gives for the statement quoted in the question. Only (a) is the theme which runs throughout the passage, and directly explains the quoted statement.

11. CHILD PSYCHOLOGY

1 **What does the author identify as the _main cause_ of the game the child is playing?**

The correct answer is (d). This question is asking you to identify, amidst a number of possible justifications for the game the child is playing, the justification the author argues for. This is therefore an argument identification question, and you should employ the detail and context methodology to isolate the **most significant** argument the author introduces, which is represented by option (e).

2 **Which of the following _comes closest_ to explaining why the author thinks that it is 'of no importance for the affective value of this game whether the child invented it himself or adopted it from a suggestion from outside'?**

The correct answer is (a). This question requires you to synthesise the passage as a whole and to interpret the author's comment in the light of this synthesis. Doing so will allow you to see that the author is concentrating in his analysis on the reasons why the child is playing the game, rather than the origin of the game.

3 **In their context in the passage, which of the following phrases does _not_ introduce a new argument?**

The correct answer is (e). This question requires you to think carefully about what is an argument and what is not, and in so doing to think about which sentences build up an argument and which sentences merely provide commentary. This is a difficult task in this passage, since the author has expressed himself in a mix of argumentative and descriptive elements. It should be clear however that the sentence begun by the phrase in (e) is merely an introductory sentence to a more substantial argument.

12. EIGHTEENTH CENTURY MANNERS

1 Which of the following is *implied but not stated* in the author's discussion of 'forms'?

The correct answer is (d). Looking closely at the relevant part of the author's discussion, it should be fairly clear to deduce from the author's opinion that *because* forms are not founded upon reason 'they are beneath a wise man's regard', he is implying that the best things to study are rational things.

2 The author uses the word 'bigotry' to mean:

The correct answer is (b). This question is complicated by the fact that the true sense of the author's use of the word is only explictly revealed from the sentences subsequent to it. Once you have realised this, it is then a matter of applying this subsequent explanation to identify the meaning of the author's use of the word.

3 Using the whole passage and applying the author's definition, which of the following is *not* a difference between good manners and good breeding?

The correct answer is (c). This question is asking you to **apply** the **argument** that the author makes in the whole passage to a fresh set of propositions. You have first to understand what the difference is that the author himself argues for between good manners and good breeding in the passage, and then apply that definition to each of the propositions the question gives you in order to see which is inconsistent with that definition; that is, which option is **not** a difference between good manners and good breeding.

PART II:
ESSAY ANSWERS AND GUIDANCE

1   **Make the best case for charging undergraduate university students the full cost of their degrees.**

This question tests your ability to draft a persuasive argument in favour of a pre-determined cause. Irrespective of whether or not you agree with the motion of charging undergraduates the full cost of their degrees, you are expected to play devil's advocate to the extent that you disagree. This is very similar to what lawyers are expected to do in their day-to-day practice. The question asks you to come up with concise and compelling points in favour of the proposals recently adopted by the government's higher education reform.

Answering this question successfully requires some general current awareness. In order for your arguments to be persuasive, firstly you have to demonstrate some knowledge of the main principles and proposals included in Lord Browne's report *Securing a Sustainable Future for Higher Education: An Independent Review of Higher Education and Student Finance* from October 2010.[3] Second, you are expected to show an understanding of how the implementation of the main principles included in the report will secure an advantage over the current system of university funding.

Some of the arguments you are likely to invoke will be the following.

1. There should be more money flowing into higher education as the current system puts a limit on the level of investment. As a consequence the UK loses its competitive advantage over other countries as a global provider of higher education.

2. By increasing the funds entering higher education institutions, student choice is given greater power in influencing decision-making by universities, as the latter can ensure that student demand is met at all times.

---

[3] The full report of the review can be found at www.bis.gov.uk/assets/biscore/corporate/docs/s/10-1208-securing-sustainable-higher-education-browne-report.pdf.

3. The removal of the current ceiling of tuition fees at £3,000, will replace government decision-making with that of student choice, which will democratise higher education.

4. The private funding of universities will provide a source of income for institutions that is no longer dependent on public spending.

5. By charging the rate of interest paid by the government, the government subsidies would be much reduced. The nature of the relationship between student and institution would be changed to one between consumer and provider, with the government acting as the bank.

Finally, the most persuasive arguments will anticipate the likely points which could be made against their cause and pre-emptively rebut them. You may wish to consider how charging students the full cost of their degree may disadvantage the current system. However, no matter how persuasive you may find these disadvantages, do not forget to reason against the arguments contrary to your case as artfully as you can in order to make your essay persuasive.

2	What is equality and why does it matter?

This question tests your ability to define a seemingly abstract concept. Secondly, the question tests your understanding of the concept's importance and how it is applied in practice. You may wish to structure your answer according to these two parts. Alternatively, the question can be answered by discussing different notions of equality and substantiating each with an example. There are a number of ways to write a successful answer. Here are some points you may choose to include.

1. There is a conceptual difference between equality of opportunity and equality of outcome. Procedural equality, or equality of opportunity, ensures that everyone, irrespective of their race, social class and sex is given the same treatment by law. For example, in applying for a job, procedural equality ensures that every applicant is given the same opportunity and consideration for the job. This tries to ensure that the most qualified person, irrespective of their race, social class or sex, will receive the job.

2. Substantive equality, on the other hand, strives toward giving each person an equal result irrespective of their race, sex, religion or ability. Its goal is to ensure that there is not only an equal chance but a proportionate treatment with respect to each person's background. In the example above, if a conception of substantive equality is applied to the selection process, a person's background characteristics receive much more prominence. Any identified disadvantage would be weighted proportionate to their qualifications. This is at some sacrifice of objective questions as to the seemingly best qualified applicant.

3. Which version of equality does our society adopt in most cases? Why?

4. Are there cases where equality of opportunity alone is insufficient to ensure that everyone in fact has an equal opportunity? How is this compensated for? Is this compensation sufficient? Is it fair?

5. What is the importance of equality with respect to achieving a democratic society? For example, is the equal right to a vote sufficient to achieve equality in light of the 'first past the post' voting system, whereby some votes prove more important than others in that they are given a greater weight?

> **3** 'The banning of outward religious symbols such as wearing the burkha or the Cross exemplifies Western society's inability to cope with cultural and social diversity.' Do you agree?

This question is very similar to the format of questions which have come up on the LNAT in the recent past. It contains a polarising statement which seeks to provoke you into a debate. The error most students make when answering such a question is to immediately list a number of examples supporting or opposing the statement, without putting forth any analysis of the issues which the statement is addressing, or considering any possible reasons why one may take an opposing view. The best course to take with a question like this is to link it to a current debate regarding a ban on outward religious symbols. For this reason, we advise you to only answer a question like this if you are familiar with the current affairs and political controversies of the matter. Otherwise, you may misinterpret what the question is asking you to debate and make arguments which are not relevant.

We recommend that you express your opinion clearly without sitting on the fence, and after due consideration of the arguments supporting *and* opposing the statement. Some of the relevant points you may wish to address include the following.

1. French President Sarkozy's proposal to ban the burkha, and other religious symbols, in public places is one of the most recent occasions in which the issue of wearing outward religious symbols has been discussed. What is the reasoning behind the proposal? Whose interests does the proposal officially seek to protect by banning the burkha and the cross?

2. To what extent would such a ban be effective in achieving the overall secularisation of public space? Is such a secularisation desirable?

3. Does the ban achieve a proportionate balance between the interests of those who wish to express their religion and those who do not wish to be influenced by others' religious views and expressions? Here it may be helpful to consider whether all persons, who express their religion outwardly, will be affected in the same way. For example, a cross may be worn under a sweater, whereas a burkha cannot be disguised so easily. Therefore, those wearing the latter may suffer a greater infringement of their freedom of religious expression than others. Is such an an infringement justified?

4. Which are the religious groups which may be most aggrieved by such a ban? What are the effects of the religious ban with respect to those religious groups? You may wish to consider the social and political response to the ban in France.

5. Finally, can a ban on outward religious symbols be said to pursue any goals other than the secularisation of the public sphere? What may those goals be? Here it may be helpful to explore France's struggle with social cohesion in light of multiculturalism and immigration.

| 4 | Critically examine the reasons for and against introducing proportionate representation in the UK. |

The starting point when answering this question is defining proportionate representation. In order to do so fully, you must also differentiate it from the current 'first-past-the-post' voting system in the United Kingdom. Next, you would be expected to give a well thought-out list of reasons for and against changing the voting system to proportionate representation. Most students will likely stop at this stage and conclude their essay with an ambivalent statement summing up the fact that there are a number of reasons for and against proportionate representation. Unfortunately, this would not answer the question because you are asked to *critically examine* the reasons you come up with in either case.

To critically examine a reason means to weigh up the extent of its influence and explain its persuasive value. For example, a reason in support of proportionate representation may be that it ensures that equality in voting is extended beyond the equal *right* to vote to the equal *weight* attached to each vote. In support of this you may add that equality in voting rights goes to the very heart of democracy and therefore proportionate representation guarantees a more democratic result in a governing parliament. Therefore if the purpose of elections is to ensure democratic governance, proportionate representation is the best means of attaining this purpose. You may wish to counter this by saying that democratic governance is the dominant purpose of elections, but democracy is not exhausted by equality in voting. At this stage you may make an argument in favour of efficient governance which must be supported by any voting system. Proportionate representation, it may be argued, poses a threat to efficiency in government decision-making because it often results in a coalition government.

As you can see, despite the very clear-cut instruction in the question to put forth reasons on either side, a critical examination requires you to consider the purpose behind each reason and weave into your argument any countervailing arguments in a way which ultimately persuades the examiner for or against proportionate representation. It is therefore difficult to write an excellent answer to such a question without seeking to persuade the reader in a certain direction. We suggest that you adopt a stance one way or the other, and from this point of view examine the reasons for and against. Some of the general points you may wish to include are as follows.

1. The current voting system in the UK results in the government consisting of a party which won the majority of seats. Seats won on a 'first-past-the-post' basis means that a party who wins the majority of votes for a seat, i.e. 50% or more, is wins the seat outright. The rest of the voters, even if their votes total 49%, would not be given representation in that seat. Thereafter, the party with the greatest number of seats, i.e. 50% or more, will hold an outright majority in parliament.

2. By contrast, proportionate representation means that each vote is given a proportionate weight in parliament. For example, if a party receives 55% of the votes, it will hold a number of seats in parliament in proportion to the total of votes won. Similarly, if a party receives 10% of the votes, it will hold 10% of the seats in parliament.

3. The introduction of a form of proportionate representation is currently proposed by the Liberal Democrat Party in the form of an Alternative Vote (AV/ AV+), whereby voters would retain a single vote for their local MP, but would have the alternative of ranking candidates first and second. The two candidates with the most votes contest an instant run-off. This ensures that all MPs can say they were supported by more than half the voters in their seat, and yet retains the current system of a single vote which guarantees that the party with the greatest number of seats will hold an outright majority in parliament. The problem with AV or AV+ is that it is not necessarily 'proportional' and it allows for great distortions in results if every seat uses AV.

4. The Labour government has also made proposals for a more proportional system than AV or AV+, but not the purest form of proportionate representation, as might be found in Germany or Israel.

It is a good idea to be broadly familiar with the policy proposals of the Liberal Democrat or Labour parties for the purposes of your argument. This will give you the ability to critically examine specific proposals and not only proportionate representation in general. For example, you may take an angle in considering how close each model is to pure proportionate representation and what the pros and cons of each are. Your answer will be better in any event if you can provide examples from recent political debates.

5	'In light of the recent financial crisis, the UK has nothing to lose by adopting the euro.' Discuss.

Before delving into a debate as to whether the euro should be adopted in the UK, you must comment on the statement presented for discussion. This way you will set out the parameters for discussion and make clear to the examiner which aspects your answer will focus on. Remember, LNAT questions are deliberately broad so as to test your ability to argue on a wide topic within a confined space both of time and text.

First, 'in light of the recent financial crisis' can be extended to mean the financial crisis commencing in 2008 and the aftermath as it relates to Europe. Alternatively, you may choose to confine your answer to the current eurozone crisis as it pertains to Greece, Spain, Ireland, and others. Second, 'adopting the euro' should be put in the context of the UK's current membership of the European Union and the reasons for the UK's withholding from extending its membership to the eurozone. Thus you will create a platform for taking a well-reasoned stance for or against the adoption of the euro under present circumstances. Please note that the word 'discuss' does not call for a narration of events without argument. You will be expected to take a position, whether it is in support or in opposition of the statement given. Some of the issues you may choose to include in your arguments are the following.

1. The adoption of the euro is not solely about having a more widely accepted currency. In principle, it is about having an interest rate policy set by the European Central Bank rather than the Bank of England. The eurozone has expanded substantially which makes it more challenging to arrive at a single set of interest rates which have a positive impact on all EU economies. What might be beneficial for German industrial output might be detrimental for Greek farmers – it can be difficult to decide in which way eurozone interest

rates should shift. Before the euro, there was a gamut of currencies which could 'slide' against each other as it was possible for the German government to move rates up and the Greek government down, if that was what was best for both economies.

2. It may be argued that because financial services form such a substantial part of the UK's economy, the high values traded on London stock and commodity markets on transactions all over the world, mean that in financial terms, the UK is uniquely positioned in the global economy unlike other European states. Hence, it is likely to be jeopardised by a single set of interest rates.

3. The financial crisis commencing in 2008 led to a significant decrease in the value of sterling in relation to the euro - on Friday 1 January 2008 the British pound was valued at 75.63 pence to the euro. This is important insofar as any arguments against the adoption of the euro relating to the higher value of the British pound are proportionately weakened.

4. Consider the extent of the UK's liability in the recent bailout of Spain and Ireland. Being a member of the EU, the UK is subject to its financial obligations to other members which are not limited by virtue of its non-membership of the eurozone.

5. German Chancellor Angela Merkel was recently reported to have made statements considering Germany's abandonment of the euro, if a new regime for the single currency is not established. This regime would entail a re-opening of the Lisbon treaty to potentially install a permanent system of bailout funding and investor losses, should the debt crises which have affected Greece and Ireland recur. In light of the focus on the 'moral hazard' which the absence of a permanent system of bailout funding creates, markets and not only governments and

taxpayers will have to share the losses if a eurozone country struggles with its deficit. Consider the extent to which the UK's financial liability will be affected in the light of this restructuring, both with and without the adoption of the euro.

This question permits for a range of arguments. These are just a few examples of topical issues you may choose to consider - both on the nature of the single European currency and how it has been affected by the recent crisis. You may add that the UK's economy is dominated to a greater extent by commodity pricing, because of high North Sea oil revenues, unlike other European economies such as Germany and France. This argument is a strong one in the case of Norway, whose parliament has voted against membership in the EU and joining the eurozone a number of times, primarily due to the high level of commodity trading from North Sea oil revenue. The UK economy has been directed differently to the rest of Europe, to the extent that a single set of interest rates to govern both is problematic. Finally, remember to discuss the statement given by the question and relate all arguments to the recent financial crisis. Otherwise you will run the risk of not answering the questions and merely stating arguments for and against the UK's adoption of the euro.

PRACTICE TEST 2

PART I:
MULTIPLE CHOICE QUESTIONS

PRACTICE TEST INSTRUCTIONS

This section is divided into 12 subsections; each subsection has between three and four questions.

You should answer **all** 42 multiple choice questions in Part I (Section A), selecting **one** of the possible answers listed for each question.

Time allowed: 95 minutes

1. THE RED ARMY FACTION

Like Gerhard Richter, Müller finally submits to his apocalyptic visions. Both artists started working in the GDR under (post)totalitarian conditions. Müller desperately tried to reinvent politics under these conditions. His critique of Stalinism at first involved a defiant return to Leninist voluntarism; after the 1950s, his despair over Soviet-style politics finally turned into a desperate fascination with the West German RAF's radicalism, which after 1989 then slid into utter resignation tinged by an apocalyptic rage. On the one hand, this sympathy for the RAF's desperate and desperately violent acts has its roots in the (post)Stalinist conditions under which Müller wrote, conditions that cemented the legacy of National Socialism, i.e., the catastrophic imaginary, and produced a peculiar utopian voluntarism among East German dissidents. But there might be something else at stake in Müller's affinity with Meinhof's "abstract radicalism".

The RAF was undeniably a post-fascist phenomenon. West German leftists acting out the failed struggles of the anti-fascist resistance – acting out in the sense of a fantasy of *not* repeating the fate of those groups *and* the compulsive desire to do just that, to repeat their deaths in the slaughterhouses of the Nazis. The RAF's "death trip" seemed to fascinate Müller, as it did many other intellectuals of this generation. But Müller and Meinhof seem to share another experience, the experience of liberation through destruction. In a 1980 interview, Müller "admits" that his writing was driven by a "pleasure in destruction and things that fall apart". He then explains this entanglement of catastrophe and creativity with his experience of 1945: "Everything had been destroyed, nothing worked." For Müller this immediate postwar moment meant living in a "free space": "In front of us was a void and the past no longer existed, so that an incredible free space was created in which it was easy to move." This is the post-catastrophic space that Müller depicts in his "Luckless Angel" as immobilising, flooded with debris. When critics condemn his plays as "depressing", Müller explained, they obviously miss the point. "The true pleasure of writing consists, after all, in the enjoyment of catastrophe." Living in the ruins of the Third Reich, living right after the catastrophe, generates in Müller's account an experience of liberation – the apocalypse as the possibility of a new beginning. Perhaps this is the historical experience that Müller has in common with Meinhof, and another factor drawing him towards her deadly politics. For the RAF's strategy of "unveiling" the West German (social democratic state) as fascist contains another fantasy: to repeat 1945, the end of the Nazi regime – and to start over again from the very beginning.

Faced with this catastrophic view of German history and the peculiar ideological, if not phantasmatic, excess of the RAF's politics, Oskar Negt accused the RAF and their "sympathisers" in 1972 of practising a form of "erfahrungslose Politik", a politics lacking in experience and utterly divorced from the everyday life of Germans. (I will return to Negt's term in the discussion of Žižek's idea of the radical political act.) Like Müller (and Richter and Meinhof), Arendt writes in the shadow of this imaginary, but she conceptualises her *Origins of Totalitarianism* explicitly against what she calls "the irresistible temptation" to yield to the catastrophic view of human history, a view that, she argues along with Benjamin, reduces human history to the history of nature, an eternal cycle of birth, decay, and death. Thus as Müller falls back on the discourse about the rise and fall of empires after the collapse of the Soviet Union, Arendt targets this discourse about the "course of ruin" in the late 1940s, making her critique of its determinism the foundation of her attempts to reinvent politics after totalitarianism.

1 In the passage, which of the following is *not* associated with the word 'catastrophe'?

(a) creativity;
(b) freedom;
(c) a reductive view of history;
(d) a progressive view of history;
(e) inevitability.

2 What is the *main connection* the writer seeks to make between Müller and Meinhof?

(a) they both lived in post-Nazi conditions;
(b) they both were optimistic about freedom;
(c) they both liked to destroy things;
(d) they both associated ruin with liberation;
(e) they both thought West Germany was fascist.

3 The writer says that both Müller and Arendt wanted to 'reinvent politics'. Which of the following best *describes* the *difference* the writer sees between them in the passage?

(a) Müller could not see beyond the present, whereas Arendt could;
(b) Müller thinks in terms of catastrophe, whereas Arendt challenges that thinking;
(c) Müller is a determinist, whereas Arendt is a voluntarist;
(d) Müller was obsessed with the past, whereas Arendt was not;
(e) Müller thinks that destruction is a good thing, whereas Arendt does not.

4 When defining periods of time in the passage, the writer sometimes uses hyphenated phrases and sometimes puts terms in brackets, e.g. 'post-fascist' and '(post-) Stalinist'. Which of the following best *describes* the writer's *meaning* when using the *latter* construction?

(a) the writer wants to be sarcastic;
(b) the writer thinks that the historical term is inaccurate;
(c) the writer means both during the period and after it;
(d) the writer means only the time immediately after the period;
(e) the writer is uncertain about the timeframe.

2. 1950s COUNTERCULTURE

Gnossos, the book's central figure, is described as "a shaggy-haired, pot-puffing product of the Great Society, an amoral collegiate hipster who loathes convention, lusts for kicks and is determined, above all else, never to lose his cool". This is followed by Pynchon's comment that the book is "hilarious, chilling, sexy, profound, maniacal, beautiful and outrageous. . . all at the same time". Anyone over the age of fifty-five or so should be able to spot anachronism and hyperbole in these statements, but I'll come back to them when I discuss why the novel is past its sell-by date.

The story is set not in the mid-1960s but in 1958; the major characters listen not to rock and roll (except for "Peggy Sue") but to blues, Coltrane, Miles, Dizzy (quoted but not identified by name), and, the latest thing, Mose Allison. No mention at all of folk music. Fariña's [the book's author] Cornell friends note that he drew many of the characters and incidents, including the trip to Cuba at the end of Batista's regime and the climactic student demonstration (protesting the university's attempt to keep unchaperoned coeds out of men's apartments), from common experience in the late 1950s. Gnossos' major set pieces, about tracking a wolf in the Adirondacks and about a demon monkey, were polished versions of tales Fariña used to impress coeds.

In Camus' dichotomy, Gnossos is a rebel rather than a revolutionary. He despises "the regimented good will and force-fed confidence of those who are not meek but who will inherit the earth all the same" (fraternity boys), but he is willing to eat their food, drink their booze, and steal their clothes. He scorns the dean – promoted because he is incompetent as a geologist – and, indeed, the whole administration, but he regards the university as "safe", a "nice little microcosm" set apart from the "asphalt seas" outside. If and when he has to leave, he plans to live on "Stipend. Grants. The Ford Fruit. The Guggenheim Vine." He sounds rather like the student leader I heard in the late 1960s who said that he'd be willing to give up American citizenship if he could get a good job with the UN. Gnossos hasn't dropped out; he's wormed in.

For a long time, he regards himself as "invisible. . . And Exempt. Immunity has been granted to me, for I do not lose my cool." In this mode, he can vandalise a Christmas crib, steal and abandon various cars, escape various perils and rumoured deaths, use drugs, rape a coed, be a welcome guest at the Black Elk Club (where he is the only white among Negroes – a sure sign of encapsulation in the period), and receive and ignore advice from professorial mentor figures. He seeks no enlightenment, however, either from counsel or from drugs.

Felonies aside, Gnossos is for much of the novel rather like an unanxious version of Kingsley Amis's Lucky Jim, who comes from the early 1950s. He wants immediate gratification – sex, something to smoke, something to drink, a position of safety rather than power. He wouldn't mind living like his favourite professors who have children with fey names, a greenhouse with exotic plants (including marijuana), and tenure. But unlike Jim, he has a peculiarly American regressive tendency. He carries as a talisman a Captain Midnight Code-O-Gram, wears a parka that is "the blanket of Linus, warmth of the woods, his portable womb", passes over *Pogo* ("something insipid in political possums") for *Peanuts*, and accepts from his girlfriend, whom he calls Piglet, the nickname Pooh.

1 Using the *whole* passage, which of the following *best describes* the writer's *meaning* when in the discussion of Pynchon's comment, it is said 'anyone over the age of fifty-five or so should be able to spot anachronism and hyperbole in these statements'?

(a) Pynchon is just trying to flatter the author of the book, and it takes maturity to spot this;

(b) Pynchon is using ideas and concepts not present in the time of the book, yet seeing them reflected in it;

(c) the writer thinks Pynchon is nostalgic for his own youth, so he likes a book from the same period;

(d) standards of criticism change, and Pynchon is using today's idea of a good novel to compliment an older one;

(e) the writer thinks that no-one over the age of fifty-five could really enjoy a novel like this one.

2 What is the *main point* that the writer wishes to make about *Gnossos* by comparing him to the late 1960s student leader?

(a) students in the 1960s were just as politically childish as the 1950s;

(b) the drop-out rate was higher in the 1960s than it was in the 1950s;

(c) both exhibit a self-indulgent element stronger than their politics;

(d) there was not as much opportunity for Gnossos as there was for later students;

(e) students always sound the same.

3 From the *tone* of the *whole* passage, which of the following adjectives do you think *best describes* the writer's attitude towards the character of Gnossos?

(a) mistrustful;

(b) sceptical;

(c) condescending;

(d) derisory;

(e) teasing.

4 In the final paragraph but using the context of the whole passage, which of the following is *implied* but not *stated*?

(a) that the programme of 1950s rebels was safety and comfort, as opposed to the more radical agenda of the 1960s;

(b) professors in the 1950s were closer to their students in attitude than they were in later periods;

(c) Americans have a childish quality absent in the British;

(d) that students in the 1950s did not exhibit the anxiety or agitation that their counterparts in the 1960s did;

(e) the kind of cartoons a person prefers is a good indicator of their maturity and political development.

3. NIAGARA FALLS

Samuel Butler has a lot to answer for. But for him, a modern traveler could spend his time peacefully admiring the scenery instead of feeling himself bound to dog the simple and grotesque of the world for the sake of their too-human comments. It is his fault if a peasant's *naïveté* has come to outweigh the beauty of rivers, and the remarks of clergymen are more than mountains. It is very restful to give up all effort at observing human nature and drawing social and political deductions from trifles, and to let oneself relapse into wide-mouthed worship of the wonders of nature. And this is very easy at Niagara. Niagara means nothing. It is not leading anywhere. It does not result from anything. It throws no light on the effects of Protection, nor on the Facility for Divorce in America, nor on Corruption in Public Life, nor on Canadian character, nor even on the Navy Bill. It is merely a great deal of water falling over some cliffs. But it is very remarkably that. The human race, apt as a child to destroy what it admires, has done its best to surround the Falls with every distraction, incongruity and vulgarity. Hotels, powerhouses, bridges, trams, picture post-cards, sham legends, stalls, booths, rifle-galleries and side-shows frame them about. And there are touts. Niagara is the central home and breeding-place for all the touts of earth. There are touts insinuating, and touts raucous, greasy touts, brazen touts, and upper-class, refined, gentlemanly, take-you-by-the-arm-touts; touts who intimidate and touts who wheedle; professionals, amateurs and *dilettanti*, male and female; touts who would photograph you with your arm round a young lady against a faked background of the sublimest cataract, touts who would bully you into cars, char-à-bancs, elevators or tunnels, or deceive you into a carriage and pair, touts who would sell you picture post-cards, moccasins, sham Indian beadwork, blankets, tee-pees, and crockery, and touts, finally, who have no apparent object in the world, but just purely, simply, merely, incessantly, indefatigably and ineffugibly to tout. And in the midst of all this, overwhelming it all, are the Falls. He who sees them instantly forgets humanity. They are not very high, but they are overpowering. They are divided by an island into two parts, the Canadian and the American.

Half a mile or so above the Falls, on either side, the water of the great stream begins to run more swiftly and in confusion. It descends with ever-growing speed. It begins chattering and leaping, breaking into a thousand ripples, throwing up joyful fingers of spray. Sometimes it is divided by islands and rocks, sometimes the eye can see nothing but a waste of laughing, springing, foamy waves, turning, crossing, even seeming to stand for an instant erect, but always borne impetuously forward like a crowd of triumphant feasters. Sit close down by it, and you see a fragment of the torrent against the sky, mottled, steely and foaming, leaping onward in far-flung criss-cross strands of water. Perpetually the eye is on the point of descrying a pattern in this weaving, and perpetually it is cheated by change. In one place part of the flood plunges over a ledge a few feet high and a quarter of a mile or so long, in a uniform and stable curve. It gives an impression of almost military concerted movement, grown suddenly out of confusion. But it is swiftly lost again in the multitudinous tossing merriment. Here and there a rock close to the surface is marked by a white wave that faces backwards and seems to be rushing madly up-stream, but is really stationary in the headlong charge. But for these signs of reluctance, the waters seem to fling themselves on with some foreknowledge of their fate, in an ever wilder frenzy. But it is no Maeterlinckian prescience. They prove, rather, that Greek belief that the great crashes are preceded by a louder merriment and a wilder gaiety. Leaping in the sunlight, careless, entwining, clamorously joyful, the waves riot on towards the verge.

1 Which of the following *comes closest* to the argument the author makes about modern travel writing?

(a) it is now more fashionable to write about people than nature;
(b) it has now been realised that people are more interesting than nature;
(c) it has now been realised that human qualities can be seen in nature;
(d) it is better to write about people than it is about nature;
(e) it is foolish to compare Niagara to human qualities.

2 In which of the following sentences does the writer use *irony*?

(a) 'Samuel Butler has a lot to answer for';
(b) 'Niagara is the central home and breeding-place for all the touts of earth';
(c) 'It is merely a great deal of water falling over some cliffs';
(d) 'But it is no Maeterlinckian prescience';
(e) 'Niagara means nothing'.

3 In this passage, the tone of the first paragraph is different from the tone of the second. Which of the following pairs of words *best describes* the tone of each of the paragraphs respectively?

	First paragraph	Second paragraph
A	Cynical	Enthralled
B	Vague	Specific
C	Journalistic	Natural
D	Argumentative	Descriptive
E	Rational	Irrational

4. PRESIDENTIAL INAUGURATION

Forty-four Americans have now taken the presidential oath. The words have been spoken during rising tides of prosperity and the still waters of peace. Yet, every so often the oath is taken amidst gathering clouds and raging storms. At these moments, America has carried on not simply because of the skill or vision of those in high office, but because We the People have remained faithful to the ideals of our forbearers, and true to our founding documents.

So it has been. So it must be with this generation of Americans.

That we are in the midst of crisis is now well understood. Our nation is at war, against a far-reaching network of violence and hatred. Our economy is badly weakened, a consequence of greed and irresponsibility on the part of some, but also our collective failure to make hard choices and prepare the nation for a new age. Homes have been lost; jobs shed; businesses shuttered. Our health care is too costly; our schools fail too many; and each day brings further evidence that the ways we use energy strengthen our adversaries and threaten our planet.

These are the indicators of crisis, subject to data and statistics. Less measurable but no less profound is a sapping of confidence across our land – a nagging fear that America's decline is inevitable, that the next generation must lower its sights.

Today I say to you that the challenges we face are real. They are serious and they are many. They will not be met easily or in a short span of time. But know this, America – they will be met.

On this day, we gather because we have chosen hope over fear, unity of purpose over conflict and discord.

On this day, we come to proclaim an end to the petty grievances and false promises, the recriminations and worn-out dogmas that for far too long have strangled our politics.

We remain a young nation, but in the words of Scripture, the time has come to set aside childish things. The time has come to reaffirm our enduring spirit; to choose our better history; to carry forward that precious gift, that noble idea, passed on from generation to generation: the God-given promise that all are equal, all are free, and all deserve a chance to pursue their full measure of happiness.

In reaffirming the greatness of our nation, we understand that greatness is never a given. It must be earned. Our journey has never been one of shortcuts or settling for less. It has not been the path for the faint-hearted – for those who prefer leisure over work, or seek only the pleasures of riches and fame. Rather, it has been the risk-takers, the doers, the makers of things – some celebrated but more often men and women obscure in their labor, who have carried us up the long, rugged path towards prosperity and freedom.

For us, they packed up their few worldly possessions and travelled across oceans in search of a new life.

For us, they toiled in sweatshops and settled the West; endured the lash of the whip and plowed the hard earth.

For us, they fought and died, in places like Concord and Gettysburg; Normandy and Khe Sahn.

Time and again these men and women struggled and sacrificed and worked till their hands were raw so that we might live a better life. They saw America as bigger than the sum of our individual ambitions; greater than all the differences of birth or wealth or faction.

This is the journey we continue today. We remain the most prosperous, powerful nation on Earth. Our workers are no less productive than when this crisis began. Our minds are no less inventive, our goods and services no less needed than they were last week or last month or last year. Our capacity remains undiminished. But our time of standing put, of protecting narrow interests and putting off unpleasant decisions–that time has surely passed. Starting today, we must pick ourselves up, dust ourselves off, and begin again the work of remaking America.

1 From the context of the passage, why do you think the writer capitalises the words 'We the People'?

(a) the writer is using metaphorical language;
(b) the writer wants to emphasise the words;
(c) the writer is quoting the words as they were written by someone else;
(d) the writer is introducing a new idea to the sentence;
(e) the writer wishes to convey a serious tone.

2 Which of the following pairs of words are *not* used as an *opposition* in this passage?

(a) 'rising tides' and 'still waters';
(b) 'hope' and 'fear';
(c) 'celebrated' and 'obscure';
(d) 'leisure' and 'work';
(e) 'measurable' and 'profound'.

3 Which of the following is *not* used to convey disapproval?

(a) irresponsibility;
(b) faint-hearted;
(c) costly;
(d) childish;
(e) serious.

4 This passage was originally delivered as a speech. The writer frequently uses repetition to emphasise a *single* point being made. Which of the following phrases - though repeated in the passage - does *not* emphasise a *single* point being made?

(a) 'for us. . .';
(b) 'on this day. . .';
(c) 'so it. . .';
(d) 'the time has come. . .';
(e) 'all are. . .'.

5. PROPERTY

Though the earth, and all inferior creatures, be common to all men, yet every man has a property in his own person: this no body has any right to but himself. The labour of his body, and the work of his hands, we may say, are properly his. Whatsoever then he removes out of the state that nature hath provided, and left it in, he hath mixed his labour with, and joined to it something that is his own, and thereby makes it his property. It being by him removed from the common state nature hath placed it in, it hath by this labour something annexed to it, that excludes the common right of other men: for this labour being the unquestionable property of the labourer, no man but he can have a right to what that is once joined to, at least where there is enough, and as good, left in common for others.He that is nourished by the acorns he picked up under an oak, or the apples he gathered from the trees in the wood, has certainly appropriated them to himself. Nobody can deny but the nourishment is his. I ask then, when did they begin to be his? when he digested? or when he ate? or when he boiled? or when he brought them home? or when he picked them up? and it is plain, if the first gathering made them not his, nothing else could. That labour put a distinction between them and common: that added something to them more than nature, the common mother of all, had done; and so they became his private right. And will any one say, he had no right to those acorns or apples, he thus appropriated, because he had not the consent of all mankind to make them his? Was it a robbery thus to assume to himself, what belonged to all in common? If such a consent as that was necessary, man had starved, notwithstanding the plenty God had given him. We see in commons, which remain so by compact, that it is the taking any part of what is common, and removing it out of the state nature leaves it in, which begins the property; without which the common is of no use. And the taking of this or that part, does not depend on the express consent of all the commoners. Thus the grass my horse has bit; the turfs my servant has cut; and the ore I have digged in any place, where I have a right to them in common with others, become my property, without the assignation or consent of any body. The labour that was mine, removing them out of that common state they were in, hath fixed my property in them.

By making an explicit consent of every commoner necessary to any one's appropriating to himself any part of what is given in common, children or servants could not cut the meat, which their father or master had provided for them in common, without assigning to every one his peculiar part. Though the water running in the fountain be every one's, yet who can doubt but that in the pitcher is his only who drew it out? His labour hath taken it out of the hands of nature, where it was common, and belonged equally to all her children, and hath thereby appropriated it to himself.

1 Which of the following comes *closest* to the argument the author makes in the first paragraph?

(a) because you have expended effort on something, it is fair that it belongs to you;
(b) because no one owns what nature has provided, using effort on something makes it yours;
(c) because you own your labour, anything you have worked on is yours;
(d) because you own your labour, only things you have tried hard to get can be yours;
(e) because you own your labour, in working on something you join it to what is yours.

2 In their context in the passage, which of the following phrases does *not* lead to a rhetorical question?

(a) 'who can doubt. . .';
(b) 'nobody can deny. . .';
(c) 'and will any one say. . .';
(d) 'I ask then. . .';
(e) 'was it a robbery thus. . .'.

3 The author argues for a *necessary link* between:

(a) consent and acquisition;
(b) force and acquisition;
(c) labour and acquisition;
(d) mixing and acquisition;
(e) God and acquisition.

4 In the sentence which ends 'at least where there is enough, and as good, left in common for others', what is the effect that this phrase has on the argument in that sentence?

(a) the phrase qualifies the argument;
(b) the phrase invalidates the argument;
(c) the phrase disproves the argument;
(d) the phrase expresses doubt about the argument;
(e) the phrase is an afterthought to the argument.

6. CHIVALRY AND MANNERS

It is now sixteen or seventeen years since I saw the queen of France, then the dauphiness, at Versailles; and surely never lighted on this orb, which she hardly seemed to touch, a more delightful vision. I saw her just above the horizon, decorating and cheering the elevated sphere she just began to move in,—glittering like the morning-star, full of life, and splendour, and joy. Oh! what a revolution! and what a heart must I have to contemplate without emotion that elevation and that fall! Little did I dream when she added titles of veneration to those of enthusiastic, distant, respectful love, that she should ever be obliged to carry the sharp antidote against disgrace concealed in that bosom; little did I dream that I should have lived to see such disasters fallen upon her in a nation of gallant men, in a nation of men of honour, and of cavaliers. I thought 10 thousand swords must have leaped from their scabbards to avenge even a look that threatened her with insult. But the age of chivalry is gone. That of sophisters, economists and calculators, has succeeded; and the glory of Europe is extinguished for ever. Never, never more shall we behold that generous loyalty to rank and sex, that proud submission, that dignified obedience, that subordination of the heart, which kept alive, even in servitude itself, the spirit of an exalted freedom. The unbought grace of life, the cheap defence of nations, the nurse of manly sentiment and heroic enterprise, is gone! It is gone, that sensibility of principle, that charity of honour, which felt a stain like a wound, which inspired courage whilst it mitigated ferocity, which ennobled whatever it touched, and under which vice itself lost half its evil, by losing all its grossness.

This mixed system of opinion and sentiment had its origin in the ancient chivalry; and the principle, though varied in its appearance by the varying state of human affairs, subsisted and influenced through a long succession of generations, even to the time we live in. If it should ever be totally extinguished, the loss I fear will be great. It is this which has given its character to modern Europe. It is this which has distinguished it under all its forms of government, and distinguished it to its advantage, from the states of Asia, and possibly from those states which flourished in the most brilliant periods of the antique world. It was this, which, without confounding ranks, had produced a noble equality, and handed it down through all the gradations of social life. It was this opinion which mitigated kings into companions, and raised private men to be fellows with kings. Without force or opposition, it subdued the fierceness of pride and power; it obliged sovereigns to submit to the soft collar of social esteem, compelled stern authority to submit to elegance, and gave a dominating vanquisher of laws to be subdued by manners.

But now all is to be changed. All the pleasing illusions, which made power gentle and obedience liberal, which harmonised the different shades of life, and which, by a bland assimilation, incorporated into politics the sentiments which beautify and soften private society, are to be dissolved by this new conquering empire of light and reason. All the decent drapery of life is to be rudely torn off. All the superadded ideas, furnished from the wardrobe of a moral imagination, which the heart owns, and the understanding ratifies, as necessary to cover the defects of our naked, shivering nature, and to raise it to dignity in our own estimation, are to be exploded as a ridiculous, absurd and antiquated fashion.

1 Which of the following words is *not* used to convey *disapproval* in the passage?

(a) bland;
(b) rude;
(c) exploded;
(d) ridiculous;
(e) absurd.

2 Which of the following words is *not* used to convey *approval* in the passage?

(a) delightful;
(b) brilliant;
(c) decent;
(d) heroic;
(e) conquering.

3 In the first paragraph, what is the *most significant* point for the author about the *change* from the old perspective to the new perspective discussed in the paragraph?

(a) formerly, people knew their place;
(b) formerly, people held up better under terrible conditions;
(c) formerly, people's attitude made the world more worthwhile;
(d) formerly, people were more free;
(e) formerly, people were more principled.

4 Which of the following is the *best characterisation* of the author's view of the value of manners?

(a) without them, humans are left to their natural and uninspiring state;
(b) without them, humans will not behave morally;
(c) without them, people will be governed worse;
(d) without them, people will appear ridiculous;
(e) without them, people will not obey the law.

7. ON THE DECLARATION OF THE RIGHTS OF MAN AND THE CITIZEN

On the subject of the fundamental principles of government, we have seen what execrable trash the choicest talents of the French nation have produced.

On the subject of chemistry, Europe has beheld with admiration, and adopted with unanimity and gratitude, the systematic views of the same nation, supported as they were by a series of decisive experiments and conclusive reasonings.

Chemistry has commonly been reckoned, and not altogether without reason, among the most abstruse branches of science. In chemistry, we see how high they have soared above the sublimest knowledge of past times; in legislation, how deep they have sunk below the profoundest ignorance: how much inferior has the maturest design that could be furnished by the united powers of the whole nation proved, in comparison of the wisdom and felicity of the chance-medley of the British Constitution.

Comparatively speaking, a select few applied themselves to the cultivation of chemistry – almost an infinity, in comparison, have applied themselves to the science of legislation.

In the instance of chemistry, the study is acknowledged to come within the province of science: the science is acknowledged to be an abstruse and difficult one, and to require a long course of study on the part of those who have had the previous advantage of a liberal education; whilst the cultivation of it, in such manner as to make improvements in it, requires that a man should make it the great business of his life; and those who have made these improvements have thus applied themselves.

In chemistry there is no room for passion to step in and to confound the understanding—to lead men into error, and to shut their eyes against knowledge: in legislation, the circumstances are opposite and vastly different.

What, then, shall we say of that system of government, of which the professed object is to call upon the untaught and unlettered multitude (whose existence depends upon their devoting their whole time to the acquisition of the means of supporting it), to occupy themselves without ceasing upon all questions of government (legislation and administration included) without exception—important and trivial—the most general and the most particular, but more especially upon the most important and most general—that is, in other words, the most scientific—

those that require the greatest measures of science to qualify a man for deciding upon, and in respect of which any want of science and skill are liable to be attended with the most fatal consequences?

What should we have said, if, with a view of collecting the surest grounds for the decision of any of the great questions of chemistry, the French Academy of Sciences (if its members had remained unmurdered) had referred such questions to the Primary Assemblies?

1 What is the *main point* that the author makes by comparing legislation to chemistry?

(a) legislation is no less difficult than chemistry, and no one advocates the involvement of all in chemistry;
(b) legislation and chemistry share a deep similarity, and the methods of chemistry are appropriate for both;
(c) gifted scientists would make the best legislators;
(d) though Britain may not excel like France in chemistry, Britain is superior in legislation;
(e) just like in chemistry, it requires very long and difficult training to be competent as a legislator.

2 In the context of the passage, which of the following *comes closest* to the *meaning* the author gives to the phrase 'chance-medley' when describing the 'British Constitution'?

(a) the process of wise development;
(b) the process of youthful or immature development;
(c) the process of development by only part of the nation;
(d) the process of unstructured development;
(e) the process of pure chance or luck.

3 Which of the following concepts are *not* used as opposing ideas in the passage?

(a) 'maturest design' and 'chance-medley';
(b) 'a select few' and 'an infinity';
(c) 'sublimest knowledge' and 'profoundest ignorance';
(d) 'long course of study' and 'liberal education';
(e) 'understanding' and 'error'.

4 The author throughout the passage compares legislation to science. What is the best description of the *nature* of this comparison in relation to the *argument* the author makes?

(a) the author makes the assumption that science and legislation are comparable;
(b) the author states the fact that science and legislation are comparable;
(c) for the sake of the author's argument, science may be compared to legislation;
(d) the author has proved that science and legislation are comparable;
(e) the author seeks to prove that science and legislation are comparable.

8. STRUGGLE FOR EXISTENCE

A struggle for existence inevitably follows from the high rate at which all organic beings tend to increase. Every being, which during its natural lifetime produces several eggs or seeds, must suffer destruction during some period of its life, and during some season or occasional year, otherwise, on the principle of geometrical increase, its numbers would quickly become so inordinately great that no country could support the product. Hence, as more individuals are produced than can possibly survive, there must in every case be a struggle for existence, either one individual with another of the same species, or with the individuals of distinct species, or with the physical conditions of life. It is the doctrine of Malthus applied with manifold force to the whole animal and vegetable kingdoms; for in this case there can be no artificial increase of food, and no prudential restraint from marriage. Although some species may be now increasing, more or less rapidly, in numbers, all cannot do so, for the world would not hold them.

There is no exception to the rule that every organic being naturally increases at so high a rate, that, if not destroyed, the earth would soon be covered by the progeny of a single pair. Even slow-breeding man has doubled in twenty-five years, and at this rate, in less than a thousand years, there would literally not be standing-room for his progeny. Linnæus has calculated that if an annual plant produced only two seeds—and there is no plant so unproductive as this—and their seedlings next year produced two, and so on, then in twenty years there should be a million plants. The elephant is reckoned the slowest breeder of all known animals, and I have taken some pains to estimate its probable minimum rate of natural increase; it will be safest to assume that it begins breeding when thirty years old, and goes on breeding till ninety years old, bringing forth six young in the interval, and surviving till one hundred years old; if this be so, after a period of from 740 to 750 years there would be nearly nineteen million elephants alive, descended from the first pair.

But we have better evidence on this subject than mere theoretical calculations, namely, the numerous recorded cases of the astonishingly rapid increase of various animals in a state of nature, when circumstances have been favourable to them during two or three following seasons. Still more striking is the evidence from our domestic animals of many kinds which have run wild in several parts of the world; if the statements of the rate of increase of slow-breeding cattle and horses in South America, and latterly in Australia, had not been well authenticated, they would have been incredible. So it is with plants; cases could be given of introduced plants which have become common throughout whole islands in a period of less than 10 years. Several of the plants, such as the cardoon and a tall thistle, which are now the commonest over the whole plains of La Plata, clothing square leagues of surface almost to the exclusion of every other plant, have been introduced from Europe; and there are plants which now range in India, as I hear from Dr Falconer, from Cape Comorin to the Himalaya, which have been imported from America since its discovery. In such cases, and endless others could be given, no one supposes that the fertility of the animals or plants has been suddenly and temporarily increased in any sensible degree. The obvious explanation is that the conditions of life have been highly favourable, and that there has consequently been less destruction of the old and young, and that nearly all the young have been enabled to breed. Their geometrical ratio of increase, the result of which never fails to be surprising, simply explains their extraordinarily rapid increase and wide diffusion in their new homes.

1 What is a 'struggle for existence'?

(a) struggling to be the strongest being;
(b) struggling for reproductive partners;
(c) struggling for limited resources and conditions;
(d) struggling to increase the numbers of one species;
(e) struggling against weather and natural conditions.

2 When the author states, 'Even slow-breeding man has doubled in twenty-five years, and at this rate, in less than a thousand years, there would literally not be standing-room for his progeny', which of the following do you think is *assumed* by this argument?

(a) that only population will increase, and resources will remain static;
(b) that resources will increase proportionately to population;
(c) that we cannot assume that resources will be able to sustain increased population;
(d) that resources will increase, but not sufficiently to keep pace with population;
(e) that humans are no more able to control resources than animals are.

3 What is the main reason the writer gives for the 'rapid increase of various animals in a state of nature'?

(a) favourable conditions leading to higher survival and reproduction;
(b) animals being introduced to new climates and territories;
(c) favourable conditions leading to increases in fertility;
(d) domesticated animals being introduced into the wild;
(e) increasing amount of plants covering animal territories.

9. BRITISH AND AMERICAN ENGLISH

Among the honorifics in everyday use in England and the United States one finds many notable divergences between the two languages. On the one hand the English are almost as diligent as the Germans in bestowing titles of honour upon their men of mark, and on the other hand they are very careful to withhold such titles from men who do not legally bear them. In America every practitioner of any branch of the healing art, even a chiropodist or an osteopath, is a doctor *ipso facto*, but in England a good many surgeons lack the title and it is not common in the lesser ranks. Even physicians may not have it, but here there is a yielding of a usual meticulous exactness, and it is customary to address a physician in the second person as Doctor, though his card may show that he is only *Medicinæ Baccalaureus*, a degree quite unknown in America. Thus an Englishman, when he is ill, always sends for the doctor, as we do. But a surgeon is usually plain *Mr.*, and prefers to be so called, even when he is an M. D. An English veterinarian or dentist or druggist or masseur is never *Dr.*

Nor *Professor.* In all save a few large cities of America every male pedagogue is a professor, and so is every band leader, dancing master and medical consultant. But in England the title is very rigidly restricted to men who hold chairs in the universities, a necessarily small body. Even here a superior title always takes precedence. Thus, it used to be *Professor* Almroth Wright, but now it is always *Sir* Almroth Wright. Huxley was always called *Professor* Huxley until he was appointed to the Privy Council. This appointment gave him the right to have *Right Honourable* put before his name, and thereafter it was customary to call him simply Mr. Huxley, with the *Right Honourable*, so to speak, floating in the air. The combination, to an Englishman, was more flattering than Professor, for the English always esteem political dignities far more than the dignities of learning. This explains, perhaps, why their universities distribute so few honourary degrees. In the United States every respectable Protestant clergyman is a D. D., and it is almost impossible for a man to get into the papers without becoming an LL. D., but in England such honours are granted only grudgingly. So with military titles. To promote a war veteran from sergeant to colonel by acclamation, as is often done in the United States, is unknown over there. The English have nothing equivalent to the gaudy tin soldiers of our governors' staffs, nor to the bespangled colonels and generals of the Knights Templar and Patriarchs Militant, nor to the nondescript captains and majors of our country towns. An English railroad conductor *(railway guard)* is never *Captain,* as he often is in the United States. Nor are military titles used by the police. Nor is it the custom to make every newspaper editor a colonel, as is done south of the Potomac. (In parts of the South even an auctioneer is a colonel!)

Nor is an attorney-general or consul-general or postmaster-general called *General.* Nor are the glories of public office, after they have officially come to an end, embalmed in such clumsy quasi-titles as *ex-United States Senator, ex-Judge of the Circuit Court of Appeals, ex-Federal Trade Commissioner and former Chief of the Fire Department.*

1   **In their context in the passage, in which of the following does the writer use irony?**

(a) '. . . and so is every band leader, dancing master and medical consultant';
(b) '. . . for the English always esteem political dignities far more than the dignities of learning';
(c) '. . . it is almost impossible for a man to get into the papers without becoming an LL. D. . .';
(d) 'In parts of the South even an auctioneer is a colonel!';
(e) 'The English have nothing equivalent to the gaudy tin soldiers of our governors' staffs. . .'.

2   **In the passage, the writer *does not claim* that the English:**

(a) are very careful with attributing titles to people;
(b) always address people by a title they actually have;
(c) adhere more closely to military hierarchies than Americans;
(d) are fond of giving titles to distinguished people;
(e) persist with titles after they have come to an end.

3   **In the context of the passage, which of the following is *implied but not stated* about the American attitude towards titles?**

(a) Americans tend to associate titles with certain positions or professions automatically;
(b) Americans are very fond of titles;
(c) Americans do not think it is important to be precise about titles;
(d) Americans have a low opinion of titles;
(e) Americans are quicker to recognise merit, and give titles accordingly.

10. WAVES

I may conveniently explain in the first place the note called 'C'; I mean the middle 'C'; I believe it is the C of the tenor voice, that most nearly approaches the tones used in speaking. That note corresponds to 256 full vibrations per second – 256 times to and fro per second of time.

Think of one vibration per second of time. The seconds pendulum of the clock performs one vibration in two seconds, or a half vibration in one direction per second. Take a 10-inch pendulum of a drawingroom clock, which vibrates twice as fast as the pendulum of an ordinary eight-day clock, and it gives a vibration of one per second, a full period of one per second to and fro. Now think of three vibrations per second. I can move my hand three times per second easily, and by a violent effort I can move it to and fro five times per second. With four times as great force, if I could apply it, I could move it twice five times per second.

Let us think, then, of an exceedingly muscular arm that would cause it to vibrate 10 times per second, that is, 10 times to the left and 10 times to the right. Think of twice 10 times, that is, 20 times per second, which would require four times as much force; three times 10, or 30 times a second, would require nine times as much force. If a person were nine times as strong as the most muscular arm can be, he could vibrate his hand to and fro 30 times per second, and without any other musical instrument could make a musical note by the movement of his hand which would correspond to one of the pedal notes of an organ.

If you want to know the length of a pedal pipe, you can calculate it in this way. There are some numbers you must remember, and one of them is this. You, in this country, are subjected to the British insularity in weights and measures; you use the foot and inch and yard. I am obliged to use that system, but I apologise to you for doing so, because it is so inconvenient, and I hope all Americans will do everything in their power to introduce the French metrical system. I hope the evil action performed by an English minister whose name I need not mention, because I do not wish to throw obloquy on any one, may be remedied. He abrogated a useful rule, which for a short time was followed, and which I hope will soon be again enjoined, that the French metrical system be taught in all our national schools. I do not know how it is in America. The school system seems to be very admirable, and I hope the teaching of the metrical system will not be let slip in the American schools any more than the use of the globes. I say this seriously: I do not think anyone knows how seriously I speak of it. I look upon our English system as a wickedly brain-destroying piece of bondage under which we suffer. The reason why we continue to use it is the imaginary difficulty of making a change, and nothing else; but I do not think in America that any such difficulty should stand in the way of adopting so splendidly useful a reform.

I know the velocity of sound in feet per second. If I remember rightly, it is 1,089 feet per second in dry air at the freezing temperature, and 1,115 feet per second in air of what we would call moderate temperature, 59 or 60 degrees—(I do not know whether that temperature is ever attained in Philadelphia or not; I have had no experience of it, but people tell me it is sometimes 59 or 60 degrees in Philadelphia, and I believe them)—in round numbers let us call the speed 1,000 feet per second. Sometimes we call it a thousand musical feet per second, it saves trouble in calculating the length of organ pipes; the time of vibration in an organ pipe is the time it takes a vibration to run from one end to the other and back. In an organ pipe 500 feet long the period would be one per second; in an organ pipe 10 feet long the period would be 50 per second; in an organ pipe 20 feet long the period would be 25 per second at the same rate. Thus 25 per second, and 50 per second of frequencies correspond to the periods of organ pipes of 20 feet and 10 feet.

1 The author criticises the 'British insularity' in weights and measures, and recommends the adoption of the 'French metrical system'. From the *context* of the author's discussion, why do you think this is?

(a) the French system is more internationally recognisable;
(b) it is a bad thing that the British have imposed their system on America;
(c) the French system is much more convenient to measure with than the British system;
(d) the French system is more easily taught in schools, because it is simpler;
(e) the British system has been interfered with by politicians.

2 What is the *connection* the author makes between vibrations and musical notes?

(a) musical notes are made by certain vibrations in the air;
(b) musical notes can be accurately measured by vibrations in the air;
(c) it is possible to approximate musical notes by manual vibration in the air;
(d) it is possible to accurately measure vibration by its musical result;
(e) it takes more force to make musical notes by hand than by instrument.

3 From the author's discussion of musical feet per second, what *answer* is the author trying to work out by using this measure in his calculations?

(a) the time of vibration in an organ pipe;
(b) the periodicity of vibration in an organ pipe;
(c) the speed of vibration in an organ pipe;
(d) the frequency of vibration in an organ pipe;
(e) the length of an organ pipe.

11. ON LIBERTY

A further question is, whether the State, while it permits, should nevertheless indirectly discourage conduct which it deems contrary to the best interests of the agent; whether, for example, it should take measures to render the means of drunkenness more costly, or add to the difficulty of procuring them by limiting the number of the places of sale. On this as on most other practical questions, many distinctions require to be made. To tax stimulants for the sole purpose of making them more difficult to be obtained, is a measure differing only in degree from their entire prohibition; and would be justifiable only if that were justifiable. Every increase of cost is a prohibition, to those whose means do not come up to the augmented price; and to those who do, it is a penalty laid on them for gratifying a particular taste. Their choice of pleasures, and their mode of expending their income, after satisfying their legal and moral obligations to the State and to individuals, are their own concern, and must rest with their own judgment. These considerations may seem at first sight to condemn the selection of stimulants as special subjects of taxation for purposes of revenue. But it must be remembered that taxation for fiscal purposes is absolutely inevitable; that in most countries it is necessary that a considerable part of that taxation should be indirect; that the State, therefore, cannot help imposing penalties, which to some persons may be prohibitory, on the use of some articles of consumption. It is hence the duty of the State to consider, in the imposition of taxes, what commodities the consumers can best spare; and à fortiori, to select in preference those of which it deems the use, beyond a very moderate quantity, to be positively injurious. Taxation, therefore, of stimulants, up to the point which produces the largest amount of revenue (supposing that the State needs all the revenue which it yields) is not only admissible, but to be approved of.

The question of making the sale of these commodities a more or less exclusive privilege must be answered differently, according to the purposes to which the restriction is intended to be subservient. All places of public resort require the restraint of a police, and places of this kind peculiarly, because offences against society are especially apt to originate there. It is, therefore, fit to confine the power of selling these commodities (at least for consumption on the spot) to persons of known or vouched-for respectability of conduct; to make such regulations respecting hours of opening and closing as may be requisite for public surveillance, and to withdraw the license if breaches of the peace repeatedly take place through the connivance or incapacity of the keeper of the house, or if it becomes a rendezvous for concocting and preparing offences against the law. Any further restriction I do not conceive to be, in principle, justifiable. The limitation in number, for instance, of beer and spirit houses, for the express purpose of rendering them more difficult of access, and diminishing the occasions of temptation, not only exposes all to an inconvenience because there are some by whom the facility would be abused, but is suited only to a state of society in which the labouring classes are avowedly treated as children or savages, and placed under an education of restraint, to fit them for future admission to the privileges of freedom. This is not the principle on which the labouring classes are professedly governed in any free country; and no person who sets due value on freedom will give his adhesion to their being so governed, unless after all efforts have been exhausted to educate them for freedom and govern them as freemen, and it has been definitively proved that they can only be governed as children. The bare statement of the alternative shows the absurdity of supposing that such efforts have been made in any case which needs be considered here. It is only because the institutions of this country are a mass of inconsistencies, that things find admittance into our practice which belong to the system of despotic, or what is called paternal, government, while the general freedom of our institutions precludes the exercise of the amount of control necessary to render the restraint of any real efficacy as a moral education.

1   Given the difficulties the author discusses with indirect taxation on stimulants, why does he think it is justified?

(a) indirect taxation on luxury commodities is inevitable, but stimulants are a non-luxury commodity;

(b) indirect taxation on luxury commodities is inevitable, and given this, before the state taxes other commodities, it should first tax those which are harmful;

(c) though not a luxury commodity, people can best spare stimulants, therefore they should be taxed most;

(d) only those who can afford it should pay indirect taxation on luxury commodities, otherwise it is a prohibition;

(e) given the state's need to raise money, indirect taxation is preferable to more demanding direct taxation.

2   While in general free, the author argues that the state of this country's institutions is such:

(a) that people can be restrained effectively;

(b) that because of disorganisation more than anything else, despotic elements creep in;

(c) that a moral education is impossible to come by;

(d) that it requires firm proof before the state will intervene paternalistically;

(e) that it often takes a dim view of the labouring classes.

3   What is the *main reason* why the author opposes limiting the number of beer and spirit houses?

(a) because the many should not be inconvenienced on account of the few;

(b) because people can always be trusted to make the correct decisions;

(c) because it is an outrageous view for the state to take that the people who frequent such houses will always abuse them, therefore they must have less freedom to do so;

(d) because the freedom of the market should decide how many such houses there are;

(e) because the case for so limiting them has not been proved.

12. POLITICS AND WAR

The War of a community – of whole Nations, and particularly of civilised Nations – always starts from a political condition, and is called forth by a political motive. It is, therefore, a political act. Now if it was a perfect, unrestrained, and absolute expression of force, as we had to deduct it from its mere conception, then the moment it is called forth by policy it would step into the place of policy, and as something quite independent of it would set it aside, and only follow its own laws, just as a mine at the moment of explosion cannot be guided into any other direction than that which has been given to it by preparatory arrangements. This is how the thing has really been viewed hitherto, whenever a want of harmony between policy and the conduct of a War has led to theoretical distinctions of the kind. But it is not so, and the idea is radically false. War in the real world, as we have already seen, is not an extreme thing which expends itself at one single discharge; it is the operation of powers which do not develop themselves completely in the same manner and in the same measure, but which at one time expand sufficiently to overcome the resistance opposed by inertia or friction, while at another they are too weak to produce an effect; it is therefore, in a certain measure, a pulsation of violent force more or less vehement, consequently making its discharges and exhausting its powers more or less quickly – in other words, conducting more or less quickly to the aim, but always lasting long enough to admit of influence being exerted on it in its course, so as to give it this or that direction, in short, to be subject to the will of a guiding intelligence.

If we reflect that War has its root in a political object, then naturally this original motive which called it into existence should also continue the first and highest consideration in its conduct. Still, the political object is no despotic lawgiver on that account; it must accommodate itself to the nature of the means, and though changes in these means may involve modification in the political objective, the latter always retain a prior right to consideration. Policy, therefore, is interwoven with the whole action of War, and must exercise a continuous influence upon it, as far as the nature of the forces liberated by it will permit.

We see, therefore, that War is not merely a political act, but also a real political instrument, a continuation of political commerce, a carrying out of the same by other means. All beyond this which is strictly peculiar to War relates merely to the peculiar nature of the means which it uses. That the tendencies and views of policy shall not be incompatible with these means, and the Art of War in general and the Commander in each particular case may demand, and this claim is truly not a trifling one. But however powerfully this may react on political views in particular cases, still it must always be regarded as only a modification of them; for the political view is the object, War is the means, and the means must always include the object in our conception.

1 **If war is called forth by policy, *why* does it not, according to the author, step into the place of policy?**

(a) because war and policy have nothing in common;
(b) because the conduct of violence is too unpredictable to supplant policy;
(c) because the course of war does not last long enough to take the place of policy;
(d) because the nature of war means that it is possible for it to be subject to the guidance of policy;
(e) because no Commander would allow war to supplant policy.

2 **What is the relationship that the author *describes* between the political objective of war and the means of waging war?**

(a) though the political objective calls forth war, the means of waging war will supplant it as a guiding force;
(b) policy must always be supreme to the forces called forth by the means of waging war;
(c) the means of waging war are unstable, and though policy must guide war, policy must adapt to the changing means;
(d) it is difficult to describe the relationship, because once begun, the means of waging war are unpredictable;
(e) it is in the nature of the fact that politics calls forth war that they will be in harmony.

3 **From the information in the passage, which of the following convictions *underlies* the writer's understanding of war and policy?**

(a) war is at least to some extent a rational and legitimate choice on the part of states to further their policy objectives;
(b) the art of war cannot ever be related to policy, but is unique to itself;
(c) the waging of war is a legitimate object of policy in itself, without any other objective;
(d) there is an ebb and flow of violent energy in war which is unpredictable to the policymaker;
(e) policy objectives are best achieved by the waging of war.

PART II:
ESSAY QUESTIONS

PRACTICE TEST INSTRUCTIONS

This section has five essay questions.

You should select and answer **one** question in Part II (Section B).

Time allowed: 40 minutes

1 'There is nothing more worthy of a young person than the study of law.' Discuss.

2 Should assisted suicide be lawful? Please state the reasons for your answer.

3 'The government should pay obese people to lose weight.' Do you agree?

4 Should the United Kingdom repeal the Human Rights Act 1998 and enact its own Bill of Rights?

5 'The violations of privacy and personal space caused by internet networks and satellite software far outweigh any benefit which may be reaped by increased social mobility.' How do you respond to this statement?

PART I:
MULTIPLE CHOICE ANSWERS AND GUIDANCE

Because you should by now be familiar with the key skills in answering Part I questions, the advice on answering in this chapter will highlight only those particularly difficult points contained in Practice Test 2.

1. THE RED ARMY FACTION

1 In the passage, which of the following is *not* associated with the word 'catastrophe'?

The correct answer is (d). This question is a good example of the relative merits of alternative approaches to reaching the correct answer. The best way to answer the question is on an explicitly textual basis. The alternative would be a kind of deductive reasoning, which would proceed as follows: you are told that Arendt argues *against* a view which 'reduces human history to the history of nature, an eternal cycle of birth, decay, and death'. The context of the passage, and what you are told of Arendt's views, *suggests* the answer is (d). By far the better approach is straightforward argument identification: (d) is nowhere explicitly associated with the word 'catastrophe', which is the criterion the question asks you to use. Any alternative approach is extremely risky, and will not necessarily be right: opposing a reductive view of history does not necessarily mean that one subscribes to a progressive view of history.

2 What is the *main connection* the writer seeks to make between Müller and Meinhof?

The correct answer is (d). The question requires you to choose from amidst a selection of true, but trivially true, answers, and wrong, and clearly wrong, answers to reach the answer which is both true and significant for the writer. Option (d) is quite clearly the argument that the author puts forth.

3 The writer says that both Müller and Arendt wanted to 'reinvent politics'. Which of the following *best describes* the *difference* the writer sees between them in the passage?

The correct answer is (b). Once again, the explicitly textual is by far the better approach. If you were tempted to answer (c), you could only have been so tempted because you inferred that because Arendt critiqued determinism she was a voluntarist - this is not necessarily true, and more important for our purposes, it is not in the passage, and you are not asked for inferences or implications in this question.

4 When defining periods of time in the passage, the writer sometimes uses hyphenated phrases and sometimes puts terms in brackets, e.g. 'post-fascist' and '(post–) Stalinist'. Which of the following *best describes* the writer's *meaning* when using the *latter* construction?

The correct answer is (c). Here, you must analyse the usage of the particular construction throughout the passage and think in terms of *consistency.* Which of the constructions is *consistent* with *all* of the instances of this construction?

2. 1950s COUNTERCULTURE

1 Using the *whole* passage, which of the following *best describes* the writer's *meaning* when in the discussion of Pynchon's comment, it is said 'anyone over the age of fifty-five or so should be able to spot anachronism and hyperbole in these statements'?

The correct answer is (b). When you are explicitly invited to use the whole passage to answer a question, try to understand what the theme of the author's argument is throughout the passage is before returning to the specific part the question invites you to analyse. Here, a consistent theme of the author's argument is the contrast between the book's secure and unambitious 1950s setting and the more radical 1960s. The author clearly thinks that Pynchon is projecting backwards a radicalism that is simply not in the book.

2 What is the *main point* that the writer wishes to make about *Gnossos* by comparing him to the late 1960s student leader?

The correct answer is (c). Hopefully, you will have picked up on the author's contrast between the anti-conventional attitudes of the two students the author mentions and their comfortable aims. Note that you are specifically referred to this discussion of the two students: you are helped by the narrow range of reference.

3 From the *tone* of the *whole* passage, which of the following adjectives do you think *best describes* the writer's attitude towards the character of Gnossos?

The correct answer is (b). This is a difficult question which tests your understanding of the strength of words. Option (e) is too weak, while options (d), (c), and (a) are all too strong. From the options given, only (b) correctly describes the writer's tone. Note also that you are asked about his tone concerning Gnossos, not in the passage as a whole.

4 In the final paragraph but using the context of the whole passage, which of the following is *implied* but not *stated*?

The correct answer is (a). It should help your analysis to recall the theme of the author's argument which you will have identified when reading the passage. When thinking about the implication of the **whole** passage, you should be bearing this theme in mind.

3. NIAGARA FALLS

1 Which of the following *comes closest* to the argument the author makes about modern travel writing?

The correct answer is (a). The fact that the author's point is one about fashion should become clear to you from the author's singling out of a particular figure (Samuel Butler) who has altered the way in which travel writing is done.

2 In which of the following sentences does the writer use *irony*?

The correct answer is (c). Irony is a quality that is almost impossible to identify when looking at a phrase excerpted in the option list. It is vital that you find the phrase in the passage itself and read the full sentence in its surrounding context.

3 In this passage, the tone of the first paragraph is different from the tone of the second. Which of the following pairs of words *best describes* the tone of each of the paragraphs respectively?

The correct answer is (d). Once again, think about the strength of words. Some answers, like the second word in (b) might on their own be appropriate, but you are asked to consider **pairs** of words. Which **pair** of words is of the appropriate strength to describe the divergent tones of the two paragraphs?

4. PRESIDENTIAL INAUGURATION

 1   **From the context of the passage, why do you think the writer capitalises the words 'We the People'?**

The correct answer is (c). This question requires quite a fine judgement about consistency. Looking at the passage, a number of the options could be accurate, but the combination of the passage's seriousness and explicitly acknowledged quotation elsewhere in the text should make it apparent to you that (c) is the most appropriate answer.

 2   **Which of the following pairs of words are *not* used as an *opposition* in this passage?**

The correct answer is (e). It cannot be emphasised too much in these questions that you are looking at the particular use that the author makes of certain words and phrases. Option (e) is the correct answer not because there is no necessary opposition between these concepts, but because the author does not use them in an opposing way.

3   **Which of the following is *not* used to convey disapproval?**

The correct answer is (d). It is important to remember that you are asked about the meaning that the writer conveys by using certain words. As a consequence, when talking about conveying approval, it might be helpful to find for yourself a core case in the passage of a word used disapprovingly - is this particular word used in that sense?

4   **This passage was originally delivered as a speech. The writer frequently uses repetition to emphasise a *single* point being made. Which of the following phrases – though repeated in the passage – does *not* emphasise a *single* point being made?**

The correct answer is (d). This question is a very specific argument identification question. Ask yourself, which of the given sentences does not advance a *new* argument, but rather builds on, describes, or qualifies an argument which has been given before?

5. PROPERTY

---

1 Which of the following comes *closest* to the argument the author makes in the first paragraph?

The correct answer is (e). The questions on this passage test more than once your ability to distinguish the correct answer from the very-nearly correct answer. Option (c) comes very close to being correct, but analysis of the exact way the author expresses himself, particularly when he says 'it hath by this labour something *annexed* to it', should demonstrate to you that (e) is the correct answer.

---

2 In their context in the passage, which of the following phrases does *not* lead to a rhetorical question?

The correct answer is (b). This question requires only that you are able to detect that one of the usages given to you is not rhetorical. A careful reading of each of the sentences from which the phrases are extracted should be enough to reveal this to you.

---

3 The author argues for a *necessary link* between:

The correct answer is (d). Once again, though (c) comes very close to being correct, it is not quite precise enough. The more specific answer given is (d).

---

4 In the sentence which ends 'at least where there is enough, and as good, left in common for others', what is the *effect* that this phrase has on the argument in that sentence?

The correct answer is (a). This is a question about the *function* which a certain phrase plays in the author's expression of his point. Of the options given you, (a) is the only option which accurately characterises this function in the context of the author's overall argument.

6. CHIVALRY AND MANNERS

1 Which of the following words is *not* used to convey *disapproval* in the passage?

The correct answer is (a). This question explicitly plays upon the fact that this is an 18th century piece of writing, in which words used may carry a meaning which is unusual for us. 'Bland' is usually a criticism in modern English, but is here used to suggest easiness, lack of resistance and harmony.

2 Which of the following words is *not* used to convey *approval* in the passage?

The correct answer is (e). The usage this question seeks to test is more contextual than historical - the author uses 'conquering' to suggest rudeness, lack of concern and violence. The word is laden with a negative sense in the passage.

3 In the first paragraph, what is the *most significant* point for the author about the *change* from the old perspective to the new perspective discussed in the paragraph?

The correct answer is (c). This is a difficult question because the author's argument is extremely rich and emotionally expressed, and it is difficult to find any single thread which appears in all of them. Consequently, your best strategy will likely have been a 'common denominator' approach – which of the options is consistent with, or is at the basis of, the expressions of feeling the author makes in the first paragraph?

4 Which of the following is the *best characterisation* of the author's view of the value of manners?

The correct answer is (a). Once again, the common denominator approach is appropriate to filter the correct answer from the many-layered argument that the author makes. Look over the paragraph once again if (d) appeared to you to be the correct answer – though (d) comes very close to being correct, (a) is a superior fit to all of the points that the author makes.

7. ON THE DECLARATION OF THE RIGHTS OF MAN AND THE CITIZEN

1 What is the *main point* that the author makes by comparing legislation to chemistry?

The correct answer is (a). Hopefully you will have taken from the writer's concentration on the difficulty of chemistry that this is the main point he seeks to draw from the comparison. This answer is complicated by the fact that, though his discussion of chemistry is prefaced by the author making explicit the comparison to legislation, the actual comparative discussion is more implicit than stated. Nevertheless, do not be distracted by the more general discussion the author engages in: the question requires you to identify only a relatively simple point.

2 In the context of the passage, which of the following *comes closest* to the *meaning* the author gives to the phrase 'chance-medley' when describing the 'British Constitution'?

The correct answer is (d). It should be clear to you from the context of the passage that (d) corresponds most naturally with the opposition between French planning and British natural evolution that the author wants to make.

3 Which of the following concepts are *not* used as opposing ideas in the passage?

The correct answer is (d). It is important to emphasise again that, though you may know from outside the passage that there is no necessary opposition between 'liberal education' and 'long course of study' in their ordinary meanings, this is not the exercise the question asks you to engage in. Remember that you are concentrating on the usage to which the author puts words and phrases. That usage coincides in this question with the ordinary sense that these phrases do not oppose each other, but this will not always be the case.

4 The author throughout the passage compares legislation to science. What is the best description of the *nature* of this comparison in relation to the *argument* the author makes?

The correct answer is (a). What justification does the author give for his comparison? None in the text. The author rather baldly **assumes** their comparability. That the author 'specifies' the argument would also be correct, but is deliberately not given as an option.

8. STRUGGLE FOR EXISTENCE

1   **What is a 'struggle for existence'?**

The correct answer is (c). The author does not in so many words state his definition of a struggle for existence – it should be clear to you however from the discussion of the natural world being able to support increasing numbers of living things that the author's emphasis in this passage on the potential for subsistence and the competition this involves.

2   **When the author states, 'Even slow-breeding man has doubled in twenty-five years, and at this rate, in less than a thousand years, there would literally not be standing-room for his progeny', which of the following do you think is *assumed* by this argument?**

The correct answer is (a). The author makes no allowance for the possibility that an increasing humanity will be capable of increasing resources far beyond the state they either are today or were when the author wrote. He simply assumes without argument that resources will remain static. This is, incidentally, a classic failing in the 'doctrine of Malthus' which the author cites.

3   **What is the *main reason* the writer gives for the 'rapid increase of various animals in a state of nature'?**

The correct answer is (a). While it is apparent that the author is concerned with favourable conditions, he explicitly dismisses increases in fertility as the reason he is looking for. Rather, you are told that, because conditions are favourable, 'there has consequently been less destruction of the old and young, and that nearly all the young have been enabled to breed'.

9. BRITISH AND AMERICAN ENGLISH

 In their context in the passage, in which of the following does the writer use *irony*?

The correct answer is (c). Once again, when you are asked to identify certain moods in the text it is crucial that you return to the context in the passage in which the phrases you are given are used. Here, the irony lies in the flat understatement of what is presented as a strangely common phenomenon.

 In the passage, the writer *does not claim* **that the English:**

The correct answer is (b). The key to answering this question is realising that in the writer's discussion of the English and doctors he includes an *exception* to his general point about exactness of titles, 'here there is a yielding of a usual meticulous exactness, and it is customary to address a physician in the second person as Doctor, though his card may show that he is only *Medicinœ Baccalaureus*'.

3 **In the context of the passage, which of the following is** *implied but not stated* **about the American attitude towards titles?**

The correct answer is (a). What is the common denominator of the American usage to titles that the author discusses? This is again a question of *consistency.* This should allow you to reach the correct answer without too much difficulty.

10. WAVES

1 The author criticises the 'British insularity' in weights and measures, and recommends the adoption of the 'French metrical system'. From the *context* of the author's discussion, why do you think this is?

The correct answer is (c). This should be clear to you from the author's apologetic tone and his explicit mention of how inconvenient the system is.

2 What is the *connection* the author makes between vibrations and musical notes?

The correct answer is (a). This question might have caught you off guard because the connection the question asks you to find is much simpler than the discussion which the author builds upon this connection. You are not asked what does the author seek to demonstrate by this connection, but only to identify the connection itself. Close attention to the question will have alerted you to the need to look for this.

3 From the author's discussion of musical feet per second, what *answer* is the author trying to work out by using this measure in his calculations?

The correct answer is (e). At two points in the passage the author states that he is attempting to find the length of an organ pipe: the answer should be clear to you, though it is important not to be distracted by the intervening discussion on units of measurement.

11. ON LIBERTY

1 Given the difficulties the author discusses with indirect taxation on stimulants, why does he think it is justified?

The correct answer is (b). The author sets out this point explicitly towards the end of the first paragraph, and your primary difficulty was probably identifying the stages by which the argument proceeds. Once you have understood the stages by which the author discusses first, taxation; second, indirect taxation; and third, the relationship between indirect taxation and 'injurious' commodities, the answer is clearly made out.

2 While in general free, the author argues that the state of this country's institutions is such:

The correct answer is (b). Again, the author makes this point explicitly; your main task is isolating the single point the question requires of you from the author's rather broader discussion in this section.

3 What is the *main reason* why the author opposes limiting the number of beer and spirit houses?

The correct answer is (c). This question partly requires you to recognise the sentiment that motivates the author's comment that the view he discusses 'is suited only to a state of society in which the labouring classes are avowedly treated as children or savages, and placed under an education of restraint, to fit them for future admission to the privileges of freedom" and partly requires you to identify the argument that is made.

12. POLITICS AND WAR

1 If war is called forth by policy, *why* does it not, according to the author, step into the place of policy?

The correct answer is (d). This passage is a slightly dated translation from the German original, and it is fair to say that the presentation of the author's style is rather dense. It is crucial therefore that you pay very close attention to what he says and what he does not say. A close reading should have impressed upon you in the first paragraph that the author emphasises that war has both its own nature yet is nevertheless an instrument of political policy. First, the author states early in the first paragraph that he considers that war is independent from policy. Then he argues against a misunderstanding of the nature of war: it is not a predetermined absolute expression of force, but has its own violent nature which can at times be unpredictable. It is this length and unpredictability which allows it to be moulded to the ends of policy. This is the reason **why** war does not take the place of policy. It is important to follow the stages of the author's argument.

2 What is the relationship that the author *describes* between the political objective of war and the means of waging war?

The correct answer is (c). This should have been apparent to you from a plain reading of the second paragraph. Though the author often qualifies the point he is making, it should help you to see his sentences develop the same line of argument in greater or lesser degrees of generality.

3 From the information in the passage, which of the following convictions *underlies* the writer's understanding of war and policy?

The correct answer is (a). This is a question of identifying a broad assumption which the author makes and is an unspoken feature of his argument. The primary danger in these questions is recognising that any option which merely reproduces what is in the passage cannot be correct: if it is in the passage, it is a statement, not an assumption. For instance, (d) is not the answer. Option (e) is not in the passage, and so could be an assumption, but it should be obvious that nowhere does the author make such a strong claim. Option (a) is in fact the unspoken assumption which the author makes; nowhere in the passage does he feel the need to justify the use of force as an instrument of policy. He is merely concerned to demonstrate the relationship **between** the use and force and policy.

PART II:
ESSAY ANSWERS AND GUIDANCE

---

1 'There is nothing more worthy of a young person than the study of law.' Discuss.

The above is an adaptation of a quote by the famous Dutch legal scholar Hugo Grotius from 1633. Note that the quote from Grotius does not call for agreement or dissent - clearly, if you find yourself in disagreement you would be in a delicate position of having to justify your application for a degree in law. Should you decide to answer this question in the exam, you should be careful about how you interpret the given statement. There are two crucial facets of the question which you must address. First, you will have to define what you understand as the study of law. Secondly, you will have to put forth the reasons why its study is of value and how it is worthy of one's scholastic and vocational efforts. Some of the points you may choose to consider before answering are the following.

1. What do we understand by the study of law? The answer to this will often stem from your understanding of what law is. Does the study of law consist entirely of learning the relevant legal provisions and knowing how they apply? Would you say that the study of law must necessarily entail a normative consideration of what the law should be? In other words, it is for you to define whether the study of law should consist solely of learning pre-existing legal norms or whether law cannot be studied properly without an understanding of what justice means and what its relationship to law is.

2. Regardless of how you choose to frame your definition of the study of law, the next component of your answer should address the importance of studying law. There are a number of ways of doing this. We suggest that you create a more broad argument as the importance of law in society and that you answer include examples from recent news. Ideally, you should employ examples regarding decisions of the courts which delineate the relationship between the courts and

legislature and show how the judiciary plays an essential role in the UK constitution. Your points will always be more convincing if you can substantiate them with relevant (and brief) examples.

3. In addition to giving concrete reasons as to why law is important and its study is worthy of any person, you may find it appropriate to remark on the motivations which led you to choose to dedicate your efforts to the study of law. We suggest you keep these short and general. For example, you may choose to highlight a famous advocate who has inspired you with their ability to stimulate public discourse. Additionally, you may comment on the skills of a good lawyer, such as advocacy, eloquence, analysis and the ability to persuade in general and why you find those skills invaluable and important.

| 2 | Should assisted suicide be lawful? Please state the reasons for your answer. |

A successful answer to this question will show both a thorough understanding of the interests at stake in a paradigm case of assisted suicide, i.e. euthanasia, and a sound sense of the role of the law in such cases. Those are the two essential elements of the question. The latter tends to be more difficult to identify and address for A level students, which is the reason why a lot of candidates who choose this question because they think it is easy are subsequently disappointed to find that they have not answered it properly. Once you have presented an understanding of the components of the question, you should proceed to present a persuasive argument for or against legalising assisted suicide. Here are some points you may find helpful for your answer.

1. Assisted suicide is currently illegal in the United Kingdom. On the other hand, suicide and its attempt are not illegal. The difference is that in the case of assisted suicide the person who is assisting is made criminally liable for doing so.

2. The issue which arises is that there is an apparent inconsistency between 'allowing' those who wish to to end their lives and concurrently not allowing them to seek assistance to do so if they are incapable of completing the act themselves. This problem is further exacerbated by the circumstance of the core case of assisted suicide whereby a person who suffers from a long, debilitating and ultimately mortal illness requires assistance to end their pain and suffering. Usually it is members of the family who want to help their loved ones die in peace and without suffering through the excruciating symptoms of a disease.

3. In such a case, the interests at stake are firstly those of the ill party who seeks help in ending their life and secondly the interests of their family members who want to end their

suffering but do not want to be prosecuted as criminals for it. At its heart, the law seeks to protect the weak through norms which safeguard each individual's right to life and physical integrity. In light of this, it is recognised that individuals who wish to end their life have a right to do so in order to end their suffering.

4. On the other hand, this right is not absolute. It is qualified by the law's role in protecting all parties in a vulnerable position, including those who are terminally and painfully ill and do not wish to end their lives but are coaxed into doing so by family members with alternative motives. It is for the protection of those, arguably most weak individuals, that the law imposes a blanket ban on assisted suicide.

5. You may choose to consider whether it is possible to devise a more proportionate response to cases of assisted suicide without imposing a blanket ban, i.e. can the law be drafted in such a way as to allow for assistance in some cases but not in others? How can this be done, if at all?

6. Further, it is open to argue that there is prosecutorial discretion as to whether each case of assisted suicide should be pursued. In other words, is it in the public interest to prosecute all cases of assisted suicide? It is likely that in most cases of assisted suicide a jury will not find an assisting family member guilty of a crime, but will consider them heroic and brave for helping their loved ones.

3   'The government should pay obese people to lose weight.' Do you agree?

The format of this question should already be familiar to you from Sample Test I. The statement put forth tests your ability to assess the merit of the proposal in addressing a health issue of national concern; to distinguish between the aim of the proposal and its likely practical consequences; and to identify the nature of the interests engaged by the proposed motion. Some of the issues you may choose to address therefore will include the following.

1. Defining the problem. Statistics indicate that around 24% of the UK population is clinically obese. You may choose to give a short summary of the extent to which obesity has affected the National Health Service (NHS) and a list of the detriments which obesity is causing both to those suffering from it and to taxpayers in general, as they are responsible for shouldering the costs of curing the host of health problems from which obese persons often suffer.

2. Expand on the proposed solution. What is the aim of the proposal? Its goal is to reduce obesity by giving a financial incentive to those who suffer from it to cure themselves and thereby to reduce the need for intervention and expenses on the part of the NHS. The interests engaged by the proposal include the interests of taxpayers who are detrimented by the substantial NHS expenses in curing obese individuals of illnesses incurred by virtue of obesity and the interests of those suffering from obesity, as summarised in the first paragraph. You may choose to add that obesity tends largely to affect individuals of lower income classes.

3. Justifying governmental intervention. You may choose to add a sentence or two addressing the liberal paternalist nature of the role of government in this regard, whereby each individual's choice to look and eat as they wish is

respected, but the government seeks to 'nudge' individuals to alter their habits in such a way as to protect their health.

4. Evaluate the likely pitfalls of the implementation of the proposal. There are a host of practical issues which arise at this stage. First, if the proposal seeks to incentivise, there is a clear question as to the possibility of fiscally incentivising those who already spend a substantial amount of their money on unhealthy food. This significantly impacts the likelihood of success of the proposal. Second, there is a question as to how much individuals should be paid in order for the proposal to actually incentivise. Third, the proposal leaves scope for the possibility of abuse by individuals who yo-yo diet around the borderline of obesity in order to keep losing weight and gaining it again repeatedly so as to continue receiving money without improving their condition.

5. What are some of the measures which the government can take in order to avoid these pitfalls? Consider how remediable some of the practical issues outlined above are. For example, could the government establish a system similar to Weight Watchers which allows for supervision and tracking of progress and permits for remuneration on this basis? How cost-efficient would such a solution be? Is this a practical solution to the current approach of the government which simply entitles obese people to seek medical help of their own volition under the NHS?

6. This question allows a lot of room for debate and permits you to take a side either for or against the proposal. It is essential that you show a thorough understanding of how the aim of the proposal may be sabotaged by the practicalities of its implementation and, additionally, how those practicalities can be further addressed.

4	Should the United Kingdom repeal the Human Rights Act 1998 and enact its own Bill of Rights ?

Most questions on the LNAT are not as specific as this one, but there is usually at least one question of this type which will require specific knowledge on a given subject and it is important that you know how to answer it. The structure of your answer is entirely up to you so long as you make it clear how many arguments you are going to put forth and which issues precisely you will tackle. Remember to take a stance and to write persuasively. Whatever your case, you goal is to persuade whoever reads your essay. Please note that in order to answer this question fully you must not only present your views on the Human Rights Act 1998 (HRA), but also address how, if at all, a British Bill of Rights can remedy the objections to it. Some of the issues you may wish to tackle are given below.

1. The purpose of the HRA is to enact the European Convention on Human Rights (ECHR) domestically and make it possible for individuals to bring Human Rights claims in national courts instead of resorting to the European Court of Human Rights (ECtHR) in Strasbourg. Note that as a member of the Council of Europe, the United Kingdom has been a signatory to the ECHR since 1950 and that UK citizens have been able to bring claims under the convention since 1959 when the ECtHR was established.

2. The HRA is arguably one of the most influential pieces of legislation to be enacted in the past century. It has inspired a great deal of criticism both as to the content of the rights it includes; as judicial decisions made on its basis; as well as rulings by the ECtHR against the United Kingdom. It is important to be able to distinguish these objections because newspapers often conflate them which makes for an unclear, low-quality argument against human rights legislation in general.

3. Politically, it has been an attractive point of debate to suggest the drafting of a domestic Bill of Rights. This is

largely due to the popular perception that the ECHR is a European document based on European values which are foreign to the United Kingdom and its legal system. It is further perceived that the judiciary of the ECtHR is not accountable, either in its expertise or through being democratically elected, and yet it has the authority to make decisions which bind the United Kingdom. Additionally, there has been wide criticism from politicians, journalists and legal academics as to the effect of the HRA in 'infecting' English law with values foreign to it such as the right to privacy which is included in Art. 8 of the ECHR.

4. Further, it is important to address how repealing the HRA will affect the United Kingdom's position within the Council of Europe and indeed the European Union. Note that it is possible for the United Kingdom to be a signatory to the ECHR, but to have its own Bill of Rights simultaneously, similarly to Germany and France.

5. Consider what a proposed Bill of Rights for the United Kingdom would include. How would this be different from rights included in the HRA? It is noteworthy that British lawyers and academics helped draft the ECHR in 1950 and the nature of the rights is largely drawn on from English common law.

6. There are number of additional points you may include in answer to this question; the ones given here are by way of example. It is important to remember, similarly to the guidance in Question IV in Sample Test I, that when you give reasons you should incorporate the arguments against your case and rebut them simultaneously. The LNAT tests your ability to structure a case. The strongest case will be cross-woven, like a basket, with strong arguments persuading the reader in one direction and also interwoven with arguments against it which are rebutted on its own terms, so that it is more difficult to make objections to it or to argue that it did not take into account certain points against it.

> **5** 'The violations of privacy and personal space caused by internet networks and satellite software far outweigh any benefit which may be reaped by increased social mobility.' How do you respond to this statement?

Similarly to Question 3 in Sample Test I, the format of this type of question tests your ability to respond to a polarised statement in a structured and well-reasoned manner. A lot of students ask whether it helps to disagree with the statement given in similar questions because it causes you to create a more robust and controversial argument. The answer to this is that it does not matter. This is because the statement you are likely to get in the LNAT is so polarised that in order to successfully agree with it will require good structure and compelling argumentation. Additionally, we advise you to take clues from the question you are given. This of course means that you have to read the question carefully. Here you are asked to conduct a balancing exercise between violations of privacy caused through information technology such as Facebook and Google Streetview and the benefit of expanded social network and the benefit of leading an advanced social life online. Some of the points you may wish to address are outlined below.

1. Google Streetview works on the basis of a satellite which catches an immediate image of any address which is put into its search. Anyone who has the address detail can view the street image of the place indicated by it through Streetview. The effect of this is that you can view houses without in fact visiting them. Of course Streetview works the same way irrespective of whether you are a burglar or someone wishing to purchase property and deciding whether to view it. The recency of the image has led to significant problems for individuals, for example, for spouses caught cheating through Streetview images.

2. Groups of individuals have collectively objected to having their property accessible on the Streetview database. The most notable example is the German city of Kiel, which successfully lobbied to have its entire address database

erased from Google Streetview. So far, Google has not entered a legal dispute on the basis of Streetview and it has been obliged to erase all requested addresses. This leaves open the fact that Streetview nonetheless dictates the default state of privacy because an individual has to take a positive step of asking to have their address erased in order to protect their own privacy. Consider the impact of this on the monopoly a company like Google has on private data without government supervision.

3. One of the most important aspects in a question on information or communication technology is that of the nature of individual choice. Consider the benefits of online networking in terms of getting in touch with childhood friends, business associates, friends and relatives and take into account the benefit of freedom of information within a certain social group. The difficulty arising when an aspect of information technology, which is apparently voluntary in its adoption, is made so widely popular is that the voluntary element of choice is diminished. Many companies and associations congregate via Facebook which makes it difficult for individuals within those associations to resist joining in. There is a powerful argument suggesting that making privacy subject to market supply and demand enables the accumulation of a critical mass which leaves little choice and protection for individuals who do not wish to join in.

4. In turn, you must consider what is the alternative to such a state of affairs? Should the law interfere and ban Facebook and Streetview? If it did, on what grounds will it do so? Alternatively, what sort of legal safeguards can realistically be imposed in order to prevent breaches of data privacy without compromising the freedom which social networks give us?

5. There are myriad examples you can use from the news
    in cases of crimes planned by way of popularly available
    satellite technology, internet chat-rooms and other social
    networks. Use any news stories you are aware of in order to
    make your arguments alive and relevant.

CHAPTER 5
MAXIMISING YOUR CHANCES

A s we have already discussed, the LNAT is not the kind of test that you can study for. It has been our goal in this book to guide you through the relevant components which you will be tested on and to advise you on how to learn to complete them successfully. As it is described on the official website of the LNAT:

'The LNAT is designed to test your intellectual abilities rather than your knowledge about a particular subject. There are no facts to learn and no lessons to revise in preparation for the test. Instead you should concentrate on exercising the relevant parts of your brain, and on familiarising yourself with the test format.'[4]

It follows that your preparation will largely involve exercising your skills in reading comprehension and verbal reasoning (for further information, see Chapter 3), as well as learning to write an essay for Part II of the test (see Chapter 4). Apart from this, there is little you can do in order to prepare for the test. Remember that the test is one of skill and not knowledge. We recommend you to be cautious of anyone purporting to teach the LNAT or the material which it covers. Having helped students prepare for the test, it is our belief that a tutor can only explain the relevant parts of the test and supervise your completion of the practice tests. Additionally, they may be able to spot the errors in your reasoning and guide you through the correct answer. That said, both of these exercises can be completed without supervision, by yourself, using this book as a guide.

In this chapter we seek to address a few of the questions you may have about the day of the test, its aftermath and effect on

---

[4] www.lnat.ac.uk/lnat-preparation.aspx

your application to read law at the universities which use the test.

HOW CAN I ENSURE MY BEST PERFORMANCE ON THE DAY OF THE TEST?

It is likely that you will be nervous on the day of your LNAT. This is not helped by the fact that there is no way of knowing what will be on the test. Take this as an opportunity to develop a comfort with ambiguity. First, make sure that you are comfortable and well-hydrated on the day. Second, the LNAT is generously timed and will allow you to take your time to reason through each answer. The test is on a computer screen and will not demand writing for the first one hour and 35 minutes – even the last 40 minutes of the test will demand more planning and structuring rather than writing. Make sure that you read each question carefully and that you answer the question asked. This is the error most students make and there is no reason to be making it when there is ample time to check over your answers. Third, think about being calm and try not to think about not being nervous. If you think about not being nervous, you will only become more nervous. Unfortunately expending a lot of energy toward being stressed will not aid your answers in any way. Nor will it help you recollect any information, because all the answers are in the test itself. Go in with a calm and relaxed mind and think positively.

WHEN CAN I EXPECT THE RESULT OF THE LNAT?

By analogy with the timing of the 2011 results, if you are taking the LNAT before 15 January 2012, you can expect the result on 31 January 2012. If you are taking the test after 15 January 2012, you will receive the result in early July 2012. The result you receive will simply be the number of correct answers you have given to Part I of the test, which is currently set at 42 multiple choice questions, spread over 12 passages. Part II of the test, the essay, is read individually by each university.

WHAT SORT OF RESULTS ARE UNIVERSITIES LOOKING FOR?

The only score you will receive from your LNAT will be for the first part of the test. The universities will therefore have a copy of your test to read your answer for Part II, but only a number score for Part I. There is little guidance given by universities as to what score they expect from the LNAT. This is primarily because the test is graded holistically, keeping in mind both the quality of the essay and the number score. Additionally, the LNAT score will be taken against the background of your academic strength and the quality of your application. There is no fixed weight given to the LNAT and different universities will utilise the LNAT result in different ways.

Part II is read individually and its purpose is to present universities with a sample of your argumentative writing. There are no set rules as to how each university uses the LNAT essay and it often depends on the admissions policy of the institution in question. In some cases, the essay will be used as a basis for interview questions if the university chooses to interview candidates. Other institutions use the essay as a means for distinguishing borderline candidates by comparing it with the personal statement and school/college report on UCAS forms.

HOW MANY TIMES CAN I SIT THE LNAT?

As mentioned in Chapter 1 (page 6) you can only sit the LNAT once in the year between 1 September and 30 June. If you sit the LNAT more than once, only the first score will be valid. If you fail to gain a place at university and want to reapply you must take the LNAT again.

CONCLUSION

Our objective throughout this book has been to explain to you that success in the LNAT follows from a practised appreciation of the skills the LNAT is designed to test. Many aspects of the LNAT can seem very intimidating: the fact that you will have no idea which texts will come up, for example, or the uncertainty of which arguments you will be expected to deal with. It has been our concern to stress to you that for all the variety in the detail of the questions which the LNAT asks, and for all the changes from year to year, the skills which are tested are always the same. The questions which aim to test these skills can be understood only by means of the skills themselves. This is why we have structured our advice on how to approach Parts I and II by breaking down the types of question by skill – such as the triplet of argument, stylistic, and interpretation questions – the better to emphasise that the questions are only the vehicles for predictably configured skills testing.

This is not to say that having read through this book you will be completely ready to sit the test. It is not, after all, a test of knowledge! Understanding how the questions relate to skills and how to maximise your performance will come only from applying this information in practice. It is vital that you complete the practice questions, ask yourself what the question is looking for, and work through the habits of thought which we have outlined. Once you have come to grips with the practice tests contained in this book, your next step should be to attempt the past papers for the LNAT which you may find on the LNAT official website at www.lnat.ac.uk/lnat-preparation/practice-tests.aspx. These are real LNAT papers from previous years, complete with a basic set of answers for the multiple choice questions. Familiarity with as many of these papers as possible will both build your confidence and reinforce to you that all possible questions which you might be confronted with on the LNAT are solvable by means of the same patterns of thought.

We have mentioned throughout that the LNAT is designed to test the skills which universities consider to be the most relevant in the study of law. While it is important to emphasise that the LNAT is not law, and that the skills which the LNAT tests are only foundational, nevertheless sitting the test will be your first step to gaining a place to read law at university. This is something you may well be nervous about, and it is worthwhile to put the LNAT in context in this regard. Law is a specialist discipline which contains its own standards of reasoning and its own techniques of argument; there is such a thing as a specifically 'legal' way of thinking about the world. Much of this is quite contingent, in the sense that the way lawyers think could be otherwise, and in fact is otherwise if you compare legal writing from different legal traditions. To put it in very general terms, the fact that English lawyers tend to think in terms of certain legal categories, for example, and argue about whether events in the real world fall within or outside of these categories might well be entirely different to how a German lawyer would think and argue about the legal significance the same real world events. Legal reasoning – and this is true of all systems of law, including those systems which are 'codified', that is, which have theoretically exhaustive legal codes – is not always entirely logical reasoning. Your study of law will immerse you in legal reasoning, and you will spend much of your time trying to think systematically about questions which do not occur in non-legal contexts. This case is being cited as an authority which dictates a certain conclusion in these circumstances. What exactly did this case decide? Is it reconcilable with this other case which looks like it also might be relevant? These questions are legal ones, with their own standards of rationality, but the process of reasoning you will use is at base logical argument. Arguing for rational and defensible conclusions will be the lifeblood of your experience in studying law, and the starting point for building these skills that are exactly those habits of thought which the LNAT tests.

From your point of view, the LNAT is not therefore just a hurdle which you have to surmount to begin the real business of studying law. Preparing thoroughly for the LNAT will itself advance you well on your way to studying law successfully. We emphasised to you at the beginning of the book that this means that you should see the LNAT as an opportunity for you to begin preparing the fundamentals of your legal studies. We should like to stress this once more, and in the following pages, in which we have provided a list of further resources, you will see that we have included as recommended reading, to broaden your methods of thinking, some books which might ordinarily be found listed as preparatory reading for university law degrees. It is worthwhile to think about the outline of these works now, not only for their interest in better informing you about law, but also for the way they present the business of legal argument. If you can have the practical application of the skills the LNAT tests in mind, you will already have met your university admissions tutors halfway. Most importantly, however, our advice here has sought to raise your confidence and to convince you that with proper thought, success on the LNAT can be one less uncertainty among the many that face you.

It only remains for us to wish you the best of luck, both for the day of the test and for the start of your studies.

CHAPTER 6
FURTHER RESOURCES

BOOKS

On essay writing

Becker, Howard S; *Writing for Social Scientists: How to Start and Finish Your Thesis, Book, or Article* (University of Chicago Press, 1986)

On critical thinking

Flew, Anthony; *How to Think Straight* (Prometheus Books, 1998)

On argument

Schopenhauer, Arthur; Grayling ed. *The Art of Always Being Right: Thirty Ways to Win When You are Defeated* (Gibson Square Books, 2004)

On general law introduction

Berlins, Marcel and Dyer, Clare; *The Law Machine* (Penguin, 2000)

Rivlin, Geoffrey; *Understanding the Law* (OUP, 2009)

On studying law at university

Barnard, Catherine; *What About Law?* (Hart, 2007)

WEBSITES

Official LNAT website www.lnat.ac.uk

Bar Standards Board www.barstandardsboard.org.uk

Law Society www.lawsociety.org.uk/home.law

Financial Times www.ft.com/home/uk Probably the best
newspaper in the UK for comment and news

UK Supreme Court Blog http://ukscblog.com/ A blog written
by practising lawyers which often provides commentary on
individual cases and on the Supreme Court Justices

Eurozine www.eurozine.com A European network of cultural
and political magazines which often features articles on
Continental European debates and controversies which are not
well-reported in the UK